## BRIGHT I

# THE GOLDEN NOTEBOOK BY DORIS LESSING

**Intelligent Education**

Nashville, Tennessee

BRIGHT NOTES: The Golden Notebook

www.BrightNotes.com

No part of this publication may be used or reproduced in any manner whatsoever without written permission, except in the case of brief quotations in critical articles and reviews. For permissions, contact Influence Publishers http://www.influencepublishers.com.

ISBN: 978-1-645420-82-8 (Paperback)
ISBN: 978-1-645420-83-5 (eBook)

Published in accordance with the U.S. Copyright Office Orphan Works and Mass Digitization report of the register of copyrights, June 2015.

Originally published by Monarch Press.
Herbert Reaske
2019 Edition published by Influence Publishers.

Interior design by Lapiz Digital Services. Cover Design by Thinkpen Designs.

Printed in the United States of America.

Library of Congress Cataloging-in-Publication Data forthcoming.
Names: Intelligent Education
Title: BRIGHT NOTES: The Golden Notebook
Subject: STU004000 STUDY AIDS / Book Notes

# CONTENTS

# INTRODUCTION TO DORIS LESSING

. . . . . . . . . . . . . . . . . . . . . . . . . . . . . . . . . . . . . . . . . . . . . . . . . . . . . . . . . . . . . .

## NOTE TO THE STUDENT

This Critical Commentary is intended to aid you in your study and appreciation of *The Golden Notebook*. Most of the critical discussion will make little sense to you unless you are already familiar with the original work. The basic assumption throughout this study-guide is that it will prompt you frequently to refer back to Doris Lessing's text.

- The Editors

## SOME FACTS

Examining a widely read author who is very much alive is different from investigating a literary giant of the past. A full book-length biography was written and published some years ago about Doris Lessing. Still it is obvious that those who know her in the flesh, in England, Africa, and America, recognize that she has not escaped the jolts and shocks of our recent world. Loving it and worrying about its present and future, she has been challenged, in spite of its complexities, to keep on writing.

As Mrs. Lessing so persuasively brings out in *The Golden Notebook*, distortion can creep into the retailing of a subjectively selected list of biographical events. Nevertheless, some basic facts are important for understanding.

Mrs. Lessing was born in Persia in 1919 where her father, suffering from certain disillusions about England, had gone after World War I. Six years later this former bank manager and his family, along with a nurse, a piano, and other treasures, were on their way to Southern Rhodesia. The fortune that was hoped to be won there from farming never materialized.

Apparently, Doris was a brilliant child with her head bent over some ant-hill that claimed her attention and imagination as she roamed, usually alone, over the sun-soaked African veld. She closed in on its sounds, its colors, its smells. Still lonely "in the hollow of the night," she bent that same head over a book. She devoured the English classics and whatever else she found to consume within the limits of the strictly provincial and non-intellectual colony. Her parents, wishing her to excel academically, sent her first to a convent school in Salisbury and then to a college.

She rebelled. After insisting on leaving home as well as school, she proceeded to earn her living as a typist. Her education accelerated.

When she was still a teenager, she married, well to be sure, but even so the union proved to be a failure. Then, after a divorce, she married again. Lessing is the name of her second husband.

The life of the very young matron in a smug upper-middle class situation - babies, friends, entertaining - there were "kaffirs" to do the work - struck her as hypocritical and sterile. She found herself either crying out against or laughing at her Rhodesian relatives. They and their blacks, whom they frequently whipped without mercy, disturbed her so much that she soon made them the subjects of stories she committed to paper. Of these she accumulated quite a collection. Many were to be published later.

It seemed to her that the whites of Salisbury, finding out that there was money to be made out of World War II and that it might be dangerous to allow blacks to learn to use guns, became more and more cruel. The only whites with any sense of social justice and a commitment to change appeared to her to be a small local group of communists. Since the blacks were still years away from economic or social rebellion, it was on moral grounds alone that Mrs. Lessing became a card-carrier. The strength of her support in behalf of the small group of tireless activists was to be reflected in her fiction, including *The Golden Notebook*, written and published long after her disillusionment with communism and other power structures had set in.

After a second divorce in Africa, Mrs. Lessing took one of her children, a small son, and set out for England by way of Capetown. She arrived in London in 1949 in which year she was thirty. The story of her arrival with very little money, and that little soon depleted by tricky Londoners, she tells in her autobiographical book *In Pursuit of the English*, published ten years later.

## EARLY SUCCESS

Close to poverty, she lived alone with her small child among the lowest of the working class, whom she describes humorously and affectionately but without any sentimentality. Somehow she managed to earn a living with her pen and was lucky enough to hit the jackpot with a novel, begun in Africa and about Africa when novels about Africa were being proliferated. *The Grass Is Singing* was published in her first year in England, 1950.

Publication of this novel led to many ramifications in her literary life. Doris Lessing, the writer, was immediately acclaimed a success. But what about the woman - her private life?

There is a myth that creeps into much of her writing, particularly the story of the novelist-heroine in *The Golden Notebook*, that applies to Mrs. Lessing's personal make-up. This is known as the Sisyphus myth - a man pushing his stone up a mountain - struggle and disappointment in succession. In Mrs. Lessing's writing the boulder can be conceived as something beyond frustration. Truth perhaps. The mountain she is trying to climb (to surmount) is human stupidity.

Mrs. Lessing was dissatisfied with *The Grass Is Singing*. It paid her well but the book was often misinterpreted. Her drive, her push up the mountain began again and took over in a series of novels called *The Children of Violence*. But even this many volumed undertaking was interrupted by the carefully planned and immediately necessary *The Golden Notebook*.

## THE GOLDEN NOTEBOOK IS PUBLISHED

Mrs. Lessing doesn't appreciate it when she is personally equated with her heroines, first, Martha Quest (the subject of *The Children of Violence* is Quest) and secondly, Anna, the accomplished but disappointed novelist in *The Golden Notebook*. To be sure, Mrs. Lessing did not mind when the literary world and the public became aware of her uncanny grasp of human relationships, her command of that portion of our lives where the real and the artificial meet. Critics praised her genius for observation, her "scorching" aphorisms, her sense of humor (*The Golden Notebook* contains a hilarious **parody** on the sex life of the swan) and her serious social commitment (people did not feel about the cross-bow the way they now do about the H bomb). But when London reviewers, members supposedly of one big scrappy family, imply that the fictional Anna's love life is Mrs. Lessing's own, the artist and the woman speak out.

*The Golden Notebook's* heroine is indeed a "free" woman but the book is more than an expression of the "new" feminism. In 1962 women reviewers said that the author was the first woman to write about female sex truthfully. This is probably accurate - certainly prophetic for now the followers are legion if often less discerning. In 1967, when much that she had anticipated was then taken for granted, Mrs. Lessing pointed out in an interview that danger lurks in taking for granted what was once considered revolutionary. With the increase in freedoms she feels that the relation one has to one's society becomes ever more important. The individual's right to this or that should rather be the right of the group. Groups are as complex as individuals. Social complexity illuminates personal truth.

## THE GOLDEN NOTEBOOK TODAY

With *The Golden Notebook* Mrs. Lessing matured into what is now called in everyday language a "gut-writer." Her perspective is visceral. Her portraits are sculptured rather than painted in two dimensions. She walks around her people. She approaches them through space. She touches. She is tactile rather than visual. (Perhaps this is why *The Christian Science Monitor* in 1962 called *The Golden Notebook* an "ugly book.")

There are reasons why one sometimes feels *The Golden Notebook* was published too early. Chief among these is Mrs. Lessing's curiosity in the realm of science and its advance. She was curious about why people are lonely, why sex is sometimes unsatisfactory, why tensions, why emotional upsets.

In August 1972 *The New Yorker* published two long profiles of Dr. Neal E. Miller of the Rockefeller University in New York with the sub-headings "Visceral Learning I" and "Visceral Learning II." Doctor Miller, with the help of the best scientific assistants and the help of enormous sums of money for laboratories and equipment, had been exploring areas which Mrs. Lessing had anticipated.

In her search for the truth about herself and other people, Mrs. Lessing has been and still is a reader of enormously wide range, including the scientific. She has been and is still against the acceptance of word pairs like conscious/unconscious, voluntary/involuntary, black/white, and that pair so sanctified in literature - good/evil.

Behavioral psychology is not a new subject to Mrs. Lessing. Like Doctor Miller, she has long felt that behavioral studies are but the groundwork of a much broader science. Pure empiricism is a delusion. Doctor Miller assigns some of our bad answers to those prejudices that go back to Plato for saying that the rational soul is higher and the appetitive soul is lower. Mrs. Lessing recognizes the animal in men and indeed women too. She challenges the assumption that men can alienate themselves from their own bodies. Body rhythms do not necessarily match clock (historical) time.

Doctor Miller believes that man can respond to several senses simultaneously so that he gets help in a complex situation.

As a scientist, he keeps trying new configurations of experiments. He keeps going (like Sisyphus) even when the immediate future looks grim. This is Mrs. Lessing's world view, the artist's view. Mankind is overdue for a scientific breakthrough about himself - if not his machines. Teaching men, says Doctor Miller, to vary their visceral response is harder than training rats. As the scientist advises long-range optimism, so does Doris Lessing. All the appalling tools that man has developed to destroy the world frighten her too, but in all her work (including her more recent sallies into science fiction) she offers Hope. The Prometheus myth, the gift of fire to man, to help him when needed, has been singled out by literary critics as applicable to Mrs. Lessing. Man is to be awarded a knowledge of his inner reality. This is what is explored in the very personal story of *The Golden Notebook*.

Mrs. Lessing is enormously interested in circadian time, body control, yoga, bio-chemistry, ESP, physical and mental experiences of all kinds, anything that seeks to advance the truth. The man of tomorrow may look upon us as we look upon the ape-men.

## UNDERSTANDING THE GOLDEN NOTEBOOK

*The Golden Notebook* is an experiment in writing the truth. A new structural technique was required. The various notebooks preceding *The Golden Notebook* are individual attempts at truth telling. The complete book took three years to be written.

Mrs. Lessing claims she started at the beginning and kept right on going. In this she is an experimental writer in an old tradition. This is not to say she is uninfluenced by the writers of the "New Novel," particularly the French, Sartre, Camus, Robbe-Grillet among others. She has cut down on but not abandoned interior monologue, omniscient-author digressions. Psychological analyses have not disappeared. Still, events and happenings are allowed to speak for themselves.

She looks at the surface of the globe and into the depths of persons. She doesn't offer the reader a philosophy but attempts to draw the reader to her own wave length. *The Golden Notebook* is a long book. It takes time to read. It is not for speed-reading. Mrs. Lessing expects the reader's mind to jump to tangential thoughts. She recognizes language barriers. Words, in structured sentences and in all the devices and symbols of poets, can still fail to transfer exact thought from writer to reader.

Mrs. Lessing knows that on occasion readers are going to feel something concerning what she has written that she never guessed they would. They are apt to find themselves day-dreaming, remembering, comparing, speculating, challenging to the point where they will find it necessary to reread, to return to the point where their minds took off on their own. Then they may suddenly realize that Mrs. Lessing's verbal currents are getting through to them. They will feel that they are no longer outsiders to the story. In consequence they will sense a denser reality. They will be learning something in their viscera. Their adrenalin inputs will increase. Their temperatures may even go up. In such an artistic experience they may have to decide between fight and flight.

## FREE WOMEN AND TRUTH

The table of contents immediately following the book's title page spells out its structure. It outlines the *Free Women* sequentially, one, two, three, four, in the repetitive subtitles of the black, the red, the yellow and the blue notebooks. *The Free Women* titles were, to be sure, more provocative in 1962 than they are today, but even then "free women" were not the essence of *The Golden Notebook*. To assume that they were is to misread.

In the opening pages, the two leading heroines, Anna and Molly (you can let your mind take off to consider *Anna Karenina* and Molly Bloom) call themselves "free women." "The point is," however, they do so mockingly and, as we soon become aware, rather sadly. Their conversation is indeed bright, relaxed, cozy. Their movements are easy and expressive. Molly is Jewish and sometimes loud. She uses her hands to communicate. Anna is brittle but we gather less cowed by the other since her sessions with Mother Sugar, their pet name for the analyst they shared in common (more later concerning Mother Sugar).

Both women are currently free of marriage. Since their divorces are not recent they have had a chance to explore the question of "freedom." Their explorations have not been entirely successful. As the reader is whetted to discover the reasons for their failures, the opening scene gets more complicated by the appearance of one ex-husband. The conversation, now in three parts, warms up, relevancies and counter-relevancies tumble upon each other. Undercurrents shift from treble to bass. The **theme** concerning the institution of marriage and "free women" expands sometimes viciously, sometimes humorously. Attendant themes, such as child failure, education, big business, popsies, street peddlers, artists, writers, actresses, drunks, surface and submerge again in a rhapsody of psychiatry and sex.

At this point we come to the essence of what *The Golden Notebook* is all about. What is the Truth? Philosophers and artists have made attempts at answers - some straight and some fantastic. In her attempt Mrs. Lessing uses the device of the notebooks. In the black she writes from one point of view, from one perspective in time. In the red she shifts, in the yellow and the blue come further shifts. In each shift there is an attempt to bring light to the Truth, to illuminate the very truth. Each notebook makes its contribution to the final notebook, the synthesis which becomes the golden notebook. This last is a novel all by itself. Thereby we have a novel within a novel - truth within truth.

The synthesis is achieved by a series of stories - often the same stories. Since it is impossible for the same story to be repeated, the additions, the changes, the embellishments conscious or unconscious, truthful or colored, provide a "plot" for the whole book. We get the first story fast and then want to know what is going to be changed. We are compelled to find out even though we are aware that we are being tricked by a literary device.

We read about an author (Anna) successful and momentarily without financial worry. She has dried up, can't write any more, so she keeps notebooks. One of these is a diary (which she won't call a diary). In it she keeps a supposedly true record, her inside private feelings similar to Kafka's actual daily attempts at satisfying his desire to describe what he was feeling, with immediacy.

In another notebook Anna "remembers." She remembers details she hadn't written down before. Sometimes she recalls dreams - dreams she had at the time of the event or later dreams that related. This is what literature students of the "new" French novel call "phenomenological reflection." This characteristic in writers can be recognized by other names. Doctor Johnson in the eighteenth century called it not reflection but "imagination." (Obviously one can only imagine something that is already grounded in one's memory or someone else's that has become part of one's own.) In attempting to reconstruct an event from memory, the "new" French writer hopes to fathom its significance, but when Doris Lessing repeats scenes from memory (or imagination) she is not interested in the importance but in its truth.

Events, elements of action, plot can be lengthened or shortened - duration can be long or short. From one perspective of time or viewpoint in space, an event deserves less time or more time. A scene gets changed every time it comes into the author's consciousness. The reader goes along. The moment is the message.

We are reminded that Beckett, in organizing his writing, used colored pencils. His work is akin to painting. The yellow goes here, the red there, then the blue. Doris Lessing uses different colors for her notebooks but her execution is not color painting. It is like sculpture whose understanding requires a moving about. Because of this motion her technique has been compared to that of a movie director. Admittedly she uses close-ups, montages, fade-outs. The comparison is, however, simplistic, oversimple. In movies it is technically possible to do two scenes at once (also in stage presentations, as Eugene O'Neill demonstrated). But in a novel, with words in sequence on a page, such simultaneity is nearly impossible. That Doris Lessing brings it off on occasion transcends any conscious interest she may have in cinema.

She has refined other structural methods, particularly those sometimes labeled "symbolic structures." Before examining these in some depth, it is first necessary to consider the introductory story, the setting of the stage as it were, that Mrs. Lessing presents us with prior to our arrival at the first of the notebooks.

In what appears to be an old-fashioned way of opening up a story, Mrs. Lessing is indeed setting a trap. Underneath the guise of traditional form, the reader is being manipulated. The opening line, "The two women were alone in the London flat," is an example. It is so Victorian that some readers of the second half of the twentieth century might call it "corny." They forget that Mrs. Lessing places this first line directly under the title heading "Free Women." In this line, which is sedentary, vague, colorless, the trap consists of the fact that this one short sentence makes up the entire paragraph. Instead of the conventional minimal three-sentence paragraph with deliberate development, we have a single statement. Its abruptness leads us at once to the next paragraph in which a conversation is interrupted. "'The point is,' said Anna..." But before we learn what they had been discussing before the telephone rang (on the landing), we are intrigued to discover who phoned and what about. Then suddenly while we are still wondering we read: "'The point is, that as far as I can see, everything's cracking up'." Hardly a Victorian opening.

In the next few opening pages, the characters are gradually spanked into life even though the "truth" about them comes later. Along with this development, the reader's idea of "Truth" suffers a few shocks. In this introduction to the drama, we learn that the two women, great friends, separated for a year, used to indulge in "what's-wrong-with-men" sessions. They had formerly lived together until Anna moved out because the man with whom she had been having an affair wanted her to have her own apartment. We suspect she had been and perhaps still was in love with him even though he had skipped off soon after she had taken the large flat. Since this arrangement was expensive she had let a room. We also learn that Molly had just returned from Europe where she had found the men more satisfying but their politics (far left) unoriginal, repetitive, and boring. Nearly out of funds she had been forced home where she managed to keep her independence by acting in small parts. To some degree she also managed to keep her twenty-year-old son, who didn't work, in small funds. We learn it was his father's phone call that interrupted whatever "the point" was. He arrives soon after.

The father, since remarried (this time not to a Jewess but to a member of a respectable, monied country family comparable to his own), has since acquired three new sons, a mansion, servants, a country home, cars, and above all, Marion, his drunken wife. Although she does not appear in the opening scene, knowledge of her existence explains a great deal. We get an introductory glimpse at this lonely woman, devoted mother, charming hostess become pathological. The familiar sequence of wife in sanitarium while husband goes a-hunting; wife, home again, catches up to him; he suggests that she take a lover; when she does,....etc. etc. All beautifully boring if the story were the point. It is not. The reaction of the two women is. The subtlety of what they say as "free women" about the marriage institution is compared to what the establishment (meaning in this case, Richard, the villainous husband) offers. His comments are far from being the old expected, sentimental cliches. His language is bald (an understatement). He fails to shock the two women. Rather they are sad at the evidence of the man's lack of understanding of womankind and sex.

His former wife, Molly the actress, puts him in his place not with words, as you might expect, but with her hands! "Her white hands spreading out, palms out until they came to rest on our knees....she now brought them together in her lap, in an unconscious mimicry of the gesture of a child waiting for a lesson....those meekly mocking hands."

"'Oh Jesus!' he said, giving up."

Meantime, Tommy, their son has been standing on the other side of the door. He enters and, with the dreariest yet most malicious comment, he destroys each of the three adults, viciously. Polite, charming, brilliantly sympathetic, he addresses each in turn. He looks in their direction but like a blind man seems not to see them. (This last comparison becomes part of the novel's symbolic structure.) His visit is brief and soon followed by his father's sulky leave-taking.

Alone once more, the two women try to recapture the spirit of their interrupted conversation, but the subject that Tommy had initiated takes over. He had said Anna was afraid that she was alone, not as a woman, which she would have accepted, but alone and unique in what she was writing. She wrote in her notebooks what she was afraid to have printed. She was lonely because she was afraid she might expose herself. The problems attending her being an independent "free" woman were drying up the serious writer. Instead, according to Tommy, they should have enriched her. The first notebook, the black, is about to begin: the basic **themes** have been sounded.

## TEN THEMES TO WATCH FOR

1. Loneliness: This **theme**, already mentioned, expands to include loneliness as a result of sexual failure.

2. Failure: This **theme**, already mentioned, goes beyond parental failure. It includes political failure (as first portrayed in the earlier books of *The Children of Violence* series and continued in the more recent *Four-Gated City* in which the earth is about to be entirely destroyed and Martha Quest dies) - artistic failure - scientific failure - medical and psychological failure (which extends into

Mrs. Lessing recent novel, *Briefing for a Descent into Hell*, sometimes labeled as "science fiction") - philosophic and religious failure - academic failure. These **themes** take on the aspect of "the courage to fail."

3. Fear: This **theme**, already suggested, concerns itself particularly with emotional learning and its physical effects. It raises the question as to whether a night-time body can handle a daytime need. Racial fear is another subdivision which increases in contemporary interest. *The New York Times* pointed out in the fall of 1972 that in South Africa blacks were not to be allowed to see the motion picture *The Godfather* and, more recently, that for economic reasons Japanese in South Africa would in the future be given the status of "honorary whites."

4. Stupidity: This **theme** stresses group stupidity as well as that of individuals.

5. Madness: This **theme** includes incipient madness as well as insanity.

6. Dreams: This is one of the most interesting **themes** because of the concept of dreaming as a learning tool and the possibility of dreams representing a "denser reality."

7. Sex: This **theme** raises many questions including what causes the sex drive and its relationship to bodily and mental health. Can the cause be the result?

8. Memory: This **theme**, already mentioned in connection with imagination, is also concerned with learning experience, prophetic memory and forced memory.

9. Honesty: This **theme**, already mentioned, is most basic because the entire structure of the novel is the result of the attempt to tell the truth. From the surface truth of each of the notebooks there comes a deep truth from their entirety. The colors of the notebooks are symbolic. The Black has to do with the past and the problem of turning fact into fiction. It also concerns the blacks and darkest Africa; The Red is concerned with Communist involvement and also, to be sure, with romance; The Yellow containing the manuscript about the novelist Ella, deals with cowardice; The Blue is the supposedly realistic notebook - the true blue which is later judged the least truthful; and finally The Golden which strives to be the synthesis of the others.

10. Art: This **theme** here, as always, harks back to what the poets have always said, "Truth is beauty, beauty truth." To point out that the notebooks are a new way (all art must be new), a new literary device giving form to content goes far on the road toward art. For a novel, any novel, including here the novel its heroine is writing, the novel within the novel, must, in order to be called art, give a reader an artistic experience.

The notebooks merely set the stage - they are, as it were, a floor plan. Mrs. Lessing has substituted "nowness" for chronology. She is not sequential - not behaviorist - but cognitive. Since each notebook is a playback of another, the reader seems to be seeing himself in a mirror or on film. He hears himself differently, as on a tape recorder. He squirms a little, is a little uncomfortable. We cannot stare at ourselves too long - no more than we can stare at anyone beyond a recognition point. We must turn our glance. Just as each notebook is a shift in time and space, so does Mrs. Lessing give a new luster to the reader's experience. Just as

Anna, the novelist-heroine, renews herself in each notebook, so does the reader. He becomes firmer and more mature like a crustacean with each new carapace.

Mrs. Lessing seems to agree with Toynbee that "civilization is a movement....and not a condition, a voyage and not a harbor."

The concept of the "quest" in her earlier books is continued in *The Golden Notebook*. The Odysseus **theme** of voyaging becomes not just a movement across space but across the reaches of the mind.

It has been said that Mrs. Lessing is "not given to indulgence in symbols." This is true only within limits because there are not a few meaningful symbols to enhance our understanding as well as enjoyment. A case in point is the "festival of insects" so poignantly described in the first of the notebooks.

# THE GOLDEN NOTEBOOK

## INTRODUCTION

If we examine *The Golden Notebook's* table of contents, we see that the series of the black, the red, the yellow, and the blue notebooks is repeated four times, each series being prefaced by the story of the free women - the story of what was happening to Anna while she was writing in her notebooks. We must remember that Anna was writing in all four books at the same time. They took days, even years, to write and during this time Anna was functioning in the world of the living where things were happening. Mrs. Lessing does not give us all the black notes at once and then all of the red and so forth. First of all we see that sometimes one notebook gets ahead of the other, so the same story, being told from a different viewpoint, gets out of phase. The reader is anxious to get on but then realizes that life goes on too. He can find out about this only while he is forced to wait for more notes in the notebooks - but of course what has happened to the writer is bound to change what she writes. (Suppose someone has peeked into your diary. Would you change?) Accordingly, the various viewpoints of the notebooks themselves inevitably undergo certain subtle alterations.

The reader gets a "feeling" of movement along with the intellectual exercise of reading. He acquires particular "feelings" about particular characters as well as a cerebral understanding of them. He also acquires a "feeling" for what the truth consists of as well as a series of definitions of the word truth.

These "feelings" are partly due to Mrs. Lessing's art as a novelist. They can be evoked only by the novel itself. No analysis can substitute.

All an analysis or study-guide such as this can do is help the reader enhance his "feeling" for the book by suggesting what to look for. As in an orchestral symphony, various tunes are repeated in different keys. Sometimes they are heard one on top of another, sometimes they run along in counterpoint as in a round, one a bit ahead of another. So it is in *The Golden Notebook*. In this guide book, however, for the sake of convenience, each notebook is treated as a whole. What tunes one is to listen for in the black notebook are put down at once. Then come the tunes of the red, the yellow and the blue. Even so, before going on to the golden notebook, it is necessary to catch up on dramatic events in the lives of Anna and her friend Molly, the free women. Only then do we proceed to the so-called synthesis, the golden, which is not, in fact, a synthesis but a symbol of a synthesis. A synthesis implies an intellectual coming together - as a result perhaps of an analysis. This it is not. It is a story all by itself. Of this, more later. First the black notebook.

# THE GOLDEN NOTEBOOK

## THE BLACK NOTEBOOK

.......................................................................

The black notebook was written in Anna's room. The pages were split into two columns - one headed source and the other, money. The reason for entries in this notebook was, it appears, that her mood was so dark, even black. By the source she was referring to her successful first novel, The Frontiers of War, which made her gloomy. Disgusted with herself for writing what was false and distorted, she was compelled to reflect upon the relationship between money and truth, between truth and untruth, between reality and art.

Her doldrums were not lessened by the salutary fact that her novel - the source - had been successful and had plentifully provided money which had given her freedom never before available. It had given her a freedom from earning a living by hack writing. It had given her a freedom to write what she pleased, in her view the truth. If she had not since written anything for publication, she had at least not succumbed to extending the false for the sake of pay. Her remuneration from her novel's publication, including translations into several languages, and the honoraria for interviews and talks could have been enormously increased had she allowed the book to be made into a film.

In the black notebook she jotted down a **parody** of a synopsis of the story for a possible movie. *The Frontiers of War* title was to be changed into *Forbidden Love*. The heroine became, instead of a faithless wife, the virtuous daughter of a cook - over whom one might drool. Anna was so disquieted by the demands for a popular scenario that she felt she was incapable of writing fiction again - this regardless of the fact that she had bubbling in her head "fifty" subjects which she could pour out to grasping publishers.

The requirements of television, the "Magic Box," tempted her even less. Instead she decided to try writing the truth about events at the Mashopi Hotel that she had fictionalized into a popular story of Africa during World War II. She wanted to write exactly what had happened.

Her notations of what she remembered we receive piece by piece because Mrs. Lessing, as has been pointed out, interweaves entries from the other notebooks as we progress. This technique contributes to our suspense. In the fourth and last section of the black notebook we are even presented with a take-off of itself in the form of a "colorless" notebook kept by a young American writer "living on an allowance from his father who works in insurance." Unconcerned about truth, this young man desired only success which in his case meant getting published. He drank too much, sometimes merely to fool others. To impress visitors from home he used marihuana (remember *The Golden Notebook* was published in 1962). Nevertheless he did succeed in getting into print with several stories. He preferred to take five hundred dollars for a porno story than money from his father who crashed through anyway because to him, too, publication meant success. His son had not wasted his time.

## CHARACTERS OF THE BLACK NOTEBOOK - THE REAL BEHIND THE FICTIONAL

Who were the real people, the models Anna had turned into protagonists, the movers of the plot in *The Frontiers of War*? Anna wrote down a description of each, one after the other, in a style that she hoped would always be objective. As readers we become fascinated because, as has been said so many times, "truth is stranger than fiction." We are trapped into thinking we are reading biography. Only much later do we realize each person so described has developed an individual **theme** and, as such, is part of the structure of this experimental novel.

First on the list of characters are young airmen transported from Oxford to the training strips of Zambesia. While waiting at college to be sent out from England, they had already acquired a mood of irresponsibility which quickened in Africa. Their dislike for each other intensified to the point where they had little in common but their uniforms. Nevertheless, they were cemented together as members of a unique group. Herein lies the **theme** of "survival through the group." Ironically, the strongest of these men did not survive.

Paul, who was to become the gallant, enthusiastic, idealistic, young pilot of *The Frontiers of War*, gave only the impression of charm. He was tall, solid, alert, and agile. He had very blue eyes. His hair was "full light gold." In manner he was deferential and polite. He was English uppermiddle class. His father was "Sir something or other." But he had - and here Mrs. Lessing develops another

**theme** - "an upper class arrogance." He mocked his comrades. He played at being a Communist but knew he was getting experience, getting to know the enemy, banking information for the time when he would return to England and take his place among the better financially-free families. He considered the other men of his mess not only socially inferior but also mentally inferior.

Paul was anything but stupid. He was witty, disillusioned, but still confident of his world. He enjoyed its incongruities. He admired primarily those who try to think things out. The Communist unit that he became a part of consisted of people who at least were readers; they were analyzers of social and economic situations. In varying degrees they were all workers and thinkers. Their intellectuality was the mortar that held them together in spite of their diverse backgrounds and capabilities.

Jimmy was the young man who became sick with fear after a day's flying. Because of his hair-breadth escapes from death, he couldn't sleep nights. (He did survive. Paul did not because of a stupid accident that was his own fault.) Jimmy was Scotch. When he drank he grew sentimental. His father was an ex-Indian colonel with a fortune that was dwindling because he wasn't "the real thing," but one who liked the Indians, went in for humanity, Buddhism and poetry. Jimmy was the same physical type as Paul. However, he was "lumpish." His blue eyes, though full of childish appeal, lacked grace. Like the others, he had played around Oxford before the war. After several experiments with sex he concluded he was truly homosexual. In Africa he was in love with Paul whom he despised. After the war and Paul's death, he married a woman fifteen years his senior who never suspected his homosexuality and on whom he became completely dependent. In Jimmy, whose situation she does not find uncommon, Lessing is here anticipating her theme concerning the institution of marriage.

Ted was the dark, hairy, lively young man, sloppy in his dress, with no money in his pockets who had made his way to Oxford by way of scholarships. Born into a working-class family, he was the "only genuine socialist of the three." His enthusiasm for music and literature was matched only by his love for all people who were "beautiful, generous and good." As a consequence, he was continually rescuing some young man from the lower ranks and making him study and learn to appreciate the arts. Although he usually succeeded, we here find him unsuccessful with his latest protege. Disillusioned and angry at himself, Ted deliberately failed his pilot test. He was sent back to England and the coal mines. Finally, his lungs affected, he married a German girl who looked after him. His Oxford connection had drawn him into the group but he couldn't stand the wranglings and bitterness within the communist party cell. Intellectual hair-splitting struck him as nonsense. In Ted, who rose above his class but was never free, Lessing mocks the hide-bound divisions of the English social system.

The Boothbys, the publican, his wife, and their daughter are typical of still another English stratum, and "might never have set a foot outside of England." They ran the Mashopi Hotel where the group went on weekends. Mr. Boothby, tall, straight-backed, heavy-set, with a protruding stomach, was indeed an ex-sergeant who had married his wife on leave. At "home," meaning England, she had worked in a pub. In Africa, still pleasant and anxious to please, she had matured into dignity. She was "a large, full-bodied woman, very plain, with a highly colored face and tightly crimped colorless hair. She wore tight corsets, and her buttocks shelved out abruptly, and her bosom was high like a shelf in front." For future reference notice the repetition of certain words - high, tight, shelf. Their daughter, when we first meet her, was a young girl bursting with sex, unrecognized by herself and by the slightly older men around her but obvious to any older female - the story of how she is rescued by a "great lout of a youth" is one of Lessing's most sensitive vignettes. The three Boothbys with their black African cook are catalysts for the explosive scenes that occur within the Mashopi Hotel. They prove to be, not types, but distinct individuals. The Boothbys hold "the line" in their color-dominated society rigorously, almost cruelly. Lessing treats them as human beings, yet, ironically, she had one of the group call them "aborigines."

Willi was the one who used this word. All white British colonials were aborigines to this non-Britisher. He was important to the group: first because he was the man Anna, the notebook writer, was living with at the time of their visits to the Mashopi Hotel. The air force pilots accepted this liaison even though Anna's beauty made it difficult for them, especially for Paul whose jealousy was obvious. Willi was older and dominant, the central figure because he alone was certain that what the members of the group were doing as active Communists was absolutely right. He was a monster at arguing; he was convincing; he could also be, as Paul enjoyed pointing out, stupid and heavy. Sometimes they laughed at his dogmatic declarations but, even so, they allowed him to be the boss. "It is terrifying," says Lessing, "that this can be true."

Willi was a German exile, born to wealth, a sophisticated European stuck in Africa for the war period. With amazing fancifulness, he invented a story of how he had killed S.S. men, which the others believed because they thought him quite capable. He was always studying, making plans, both short and long-term. He put up with people he despised because they might become useful later. Anna hated him. The two lived together but did not enjoy sleeping together. They pitied each other. Each felt helpless to make the other happy. Because Anna remained in this situation long after she should have pulled out, she analyzed herself as having been weak - a word she had never attributed to herself. She apologized to herself by saying she was sexually inexperienced at the time. She had slept before only with her former husband, briefly. In this affair between Willi and Anna, Lessing delves deeper into her thesis is concerning the importance of sexual relationships - a thesis which is enlarged in the stories of two very important members of the group, in the stories of Maryrose and George Hounslow.

Maryrose was a native African white colonial. "A tiny slender girl, with waves of honey-colored hair and great brown eyes," she attracted men as a loadstone attracts iron. A male was always nearby. And Ted, already suffering because of his young protege's refusal to be rescued, would sit by her and put his arm around her. She was like so many pretty girls who allow themselves to be petted in payment, as it were, for being born attractive. Her tolerance of the adoring male was sleepy. But, as Lessing points out, Maryrose had another side.

George Hounslow is the character Lessing utilizes to pull her theme together. He is a hardworking African farmer living on his land, struggling with his black laborers, not making it much above poverty. Knowing all the problems attendant to the color line, he was drawn to the group and their communism, even to Willi's dialectic, because he was a conscience-stricken white. As a man too he had to get out from under his own roof with its squabbling old folks, his and his wife's, his children and their drudging mother whom we feel he continued to love in his own fashion. Endowed with a massive sexuality, he needed other satisfactions. He could not help bullying a woman, any woman, with his deepset brown eyes. When he fixed his soft stare upon a woman she would imagine he was looking at her with eyes he used not before but after he had been in bed with her. He was an extreme sensualist yet affectionate and civilized.

He never played the role of masculinity. Simply, his need was great. "And men," says Lessing, "can no longer dominate women in this way without feeling guilty about it. Or very few of them." George had been driving his caravan over to the Mashopi Hotel long before the group found it and made it their sinister haven of relaxation. He had, previously, fallen in love with the black wife of the Boothby's black cook.

His moral dilemma, so imposed in the color-oriented society, had been the subject of Anna's success, *The Frontiers of War*. In this notebook, however, Anna tried to recapture the facts, not the romanticized fiction, which had brought fame and money and which film and television agents were still scrambling for.

Jackson was the black cook whom George made a cuckold. These two men, despite, or perhaps because of, their situations, were the most sympathetic of the group, surely the only two endowed with a certain nobility. We first meet Jackson in connection with Mrs. Boothby whose intolerance insisted that the young air pilots stay out of her kitchen. Paul had intruded there, and one night Jimmy, who was already disliked by Mrs. Boothby because she suspected his homosexuality, an abnormality on a par with blackness, was found drunk on the kitchen floor. Jackson was trying to bring him around, and Jimmy was exploiting the situation sexually. Mrs. Boothby witnessed the scene, overheard Jimmy's drunken mumbling, and fired Jackson on the spot regardless of the fact that her cook had served her faithfully for many years. Losing his job also meant losing his home because Jackson had lived with his several children in a shack out back. Since African laborers were not supposed to live on white-owned premises but in villages of their own, Jackson and his family had to face a long terrifying journey. Involved was still another tragedy. Among the Jackson children was one much lighter-skinned than the others: George could recognize his own son. If George, a dissident socialist who took to platforms to make speeches denouncing the color bar, were to rescue his own child from Jackson's miserable slum, then George, though white, would also lose his farm. His three legitimate children would be ostracized at school not because their half-brother was illegitimate but because he was black. George grieved for this child of his. He talked to Willi about making a test case over the child. After Jackson's dismissal the young week-enders were saddened and even more disillusioned. They knew the futility of what they had been trying to do for the black man.

## THE GROUP

Anna's book *The Frontiers of War* had been just one of a spate of books published in London where there was growing sympathy for the black man and aversion to the white Africans' cruelty. That she hadn't been strong enough in her treatment depressed Anna but, looking at the group in retrospect, she realized what a mountain they had been up against. Even today we cannot pick up a copy of the British newspaper *The Guardian* without being shocked by still another example of stupid ruthlessness in Africa.

Not so much with its members but with the group as a whole does Lessing advance her political **theme**. That the group could not draw the African masses into reform they were too close to the scene to see. Black trade unions were illegal and the black masses were not yet ready for illegal action. Study classes for sympathetic whites hoping to instruct the blacks, wide reading in socialist and Communist literature, discussions till four or five in the morning were routine but ineffective. Fights within the party, hypocrisy, directives that were long out of date, had split their own group off from the official Communist line. Their responsibility shifted from that of a reform crusade to a desire to help anyone in any sort of trouble. Theirs was a Christian ethic indeed and yet nary a word about religious belief or its practice was heard among them. Theirs was a brotherhood in individualistic diversity. Did this mean anything? Or was the group just a bit mad? They were so psychologically taut that a small event like Willi's clearing his throat could strike them funny. It was bad theatre that could set them off laughing, first singly, then in couples. Suddenly everybody would be wildly laughing. The hysteria frightened them.

## THEME THROUGH SYMBOL

After having been introduced to the characters who have suggested certain themes, we return to them in later observations of the black notebook. The characters are again revealed but from a different perspective. Also the reader's perspective has perhaps altered for he has read by this time the first sections of the other notebooks. We are aware that Anna's personal perspective has also changed as the result of an unusual dream. (As we shall see, dreams are psychologically and scientifically, as well as artistically, important in Lessing's writing.) In this case, the utilization of a dream in the search for truth is not accidental. The circumstances at the time of dreaming and the dream itself are both carefully recorded. They cast new beams and shadows upon the young airmen and their friends at Mashopi. In Anna's recall they add a further dimension, the thesis that anger is dishonest.

The **episode** that seemed to trigger the dream concerned a pigeon a long way from the African veld - "a fat domestic London pigeon waddling among the boots and shoes of people hurrying for a bus." A man kicked it and immediately a red-faced woman screamed at him. She believed he had killed it but the pigeon, struggling to lift its head and give its wings a flutter, still had life. A crowd gathered. Someone said: "Call the RSPCA." A couple of boys, brazen and tough, shouted that the man belonged in prison - should be flogged. Because the hoodlums were so derisive, the woman's anger turned from the kicker to them. She forgot the bird until someone in the crowd said, "It's going to die." It did. While the kicker was protesting that his kick had been an accident because he had never before known a pigeon not to move out of the way, the crowd dissolved. The rowdies, continuing their scoffing, suggested a pigeon pie be made, but at the idea that the coppers be called, they lurched off. Meanwhile, as the dead pigeon was about to be put in a rubbish bin, the woman, her anger turned to tenderness, grasped it. "I'll bury the poor little bird in my window box."

This sketch, which Lessing presents as only an artist can, with excitement, strength, economy, gives us some insight into the human complexities Anna was trying to express in her notebook. One never doubts that the story, expressed in lower-class slang, was based on fact. Anna's recording of it belies the fact that she was supposed to be a "dried up" novelist. She was so upset by the happening that the cracking currents in her brain carried over into the subconscious world. Her notebook entry begins: "Last night I dreamed of the pigeon. It reminded me of something. I didn't know what. In my dream I was fighting to remember. Yet when I woke up I knew what it was - an incident from the Mashopi Hotel weekends. I haven't thought of it for years... I am again exasperated because my brain contains so much that is locked up and unreachable, unless by stroke of luck, there is an incident like yesterday's." It is what is "unreachable" in the human mind that is Lessing's concern. This is probably the main **theme** of *The Golden Notebook*.

It dwarfs the "free woman" concept that some hasty reviewers tried to ballyhoo.

The dream forced Anna to catapult a story out of the reaches of her memory which in turn compelled her to change her analyses of the individuals in the group and what transpired at the Mashopi Hotel. The figures of Paul and Jimmy, in particular, are approached from a different angle of elevation. In presenting the new version, Lessing benefitted from her past experience as a novelist and manifested that she was not above borrowing techniques from the movies in order to weave together in one **episode** several **themes** she had merely anticipated earlier. The story becomes symbolic.

## BUTTERFLIES, GRASSHOPPERS, ANT-EATERS, AND PIGEONS

**Irony** is the keynote of the opening lines of this African **episode**. Mrs. Boothby, having suggested that Mr. Boothby would like a pigeon pie, handed Paul a rifle. In opting to give it to Paul she showed that she recognized him as the aristocrat of the group from the hunting class. He picked up the not unflattering implication with pleasant and carelessly winning arrogance by saying he had indeed shot grouse and pheasant but never with a rifle. She said it was easy enough and that in a small vlei (a low-lying depression where water collects in the wet season) between the kopjes (hillocks or heaps of granite boulders) plenty of pigeons would settle and one could easily pick them off one by one. Jimmy claimed that this was not sporting.

In remembering Jimmy's objection, Anna was revealing a Jimmy, though outwardly still fattish and clumsy, as inwardly fastidious. First of all the Scottish gentry in the blood of his ancestors, probably as distinguished as Paul's, came to light and secondly, his domination by Paul did not prevent sudden outbursts of spirit. Lastly, Anna recalled Jimmy's look which she described as "owlish." Perhaps she was merely picturing a round wide-eyed look. On the other hand owls are identified with wisdom. In the earlier characterizations Jimmy was never shown to be wise. If we recall that the owl is also a bird of prey, the **irony** becomes obvious and becomes more pointed in the later events of that bloody morning.

In her next remark Mrs. Boothby was in character, the essence of which has not changed from what we have already come to feel. In this consistency, Lessing is telling us that it is easier to be honest about the Boothbys of the world than the Jimmies. The Boothbys may be as complicated and individualistic but, numbers being on their side, their similarities are more obvious. In diversity there is uniformity, especially in South Africa.

After Jimmy's serious remark Paul did a bit of play-acting, "clutching at his brow with one hand and holding the rifle away from him with the other." His body language reveals the falsity of his modesty.

Recovering from this mockery, Mrs. Boothby explains that there is no harm in bringing down the pigeons if one shoots to kill. The **irony** is not lost that this woman, representative of a class of whites who whipped and tortured the blacks without killing them (except by accident), had nevertheless a "sporting" instinct. And Jimmy, taking the lead again from Paul, says, "She's right." Paul merely echoes: "You're right....dead right." The "dead" in the **cliche** "dead right" is ominous.

The five of them set out. Besides Jimmy and Paul with the rifle, there were Maryrose, Willy, and Anna the "I" of this morning's story which embraces some of Lessing's finest descriptive writing.

**All that country was high-lying sandveld, undulating, broken sharply here and there by kopjes. When it rained the soil seemed to offer resistance, not welcome. The water danced and drummed in a fury of white drops to a height of two or three feet over the hard soil, but an hour after the storm, it was already dry again and the gullies and vleis were running high and noisy.**

There follows a description of what is called "a festival of insects." There are a million white butterflies with greenish white wings as though just out of chrysalises, and more millions of bright, paint-box colored grasshoppers in couples.

"And one grasshopper jumped on the other grasshopper's back." Their coupling cries itself into an obscenity just because there were so many couples. Their jerking and toppling, their staring "black blank" eyes, set Jimmy to laughing. Objecting, Maryrose said it would be better to watch the butterflies. With characteristic acuteness Paul recognized the difference in the two reactions. Jimmy saw a joy in the grotesque motions of sex, and with grasshoppers he couldn't tell male from female, whereas Maryrose in seeing no joy was unconsciously reverting to stupidity because, as Paul pointed out, the lovely butterflies she preferred to watch, were engaging in the same activity. Paul announced that he was going to try a small scientific experiment. With a tiny bit of grass, he attempted to rearrange a mismatched pair of grasshoppers. The big one being on top of the small one, he wanted the heavier weighted one to do the supporting. Having difficulties, he enlisted a second pair of sticks manipulated by Jimmy whose "face was wrenched with loathing." Despite Jimmy's awkwardness, Paul finally succeeded in maneuvering two large grasshoppers and two small ones into two well-matched couples. "'There,' said Paul, 'that's the scientific approach.'" Then Jimmy, recognizing Paul's stupidity for surely the other thousands of grasshoppers were getting along quite well without outside help, breathlessly commented, "There is no evidence that in what we refer to as nature things are any better-ordered than they are with us." Paul could have made the speech with more grace but Jimmy is growing under the reader's skin.

After watching nature at its most prodigal, each of the five knowing that before night these insects would all be dead by killing each other, by fighting, by biting, by suicide, or by clumsy copulation, they moved on under the "sucking, splendid, menacing heat." Close to a kopje a pigeon cooed from a large tree. "It was a soft, somnolent drugging sound." The noise is "like having malaria and being full of quinine, an insane incessant shrilling noise that seems to come out of the ear drums. Soon one doesn't hear it, as one ceases to hear the fevered shrilling of quinine in the blood." In bringing in the peculiar sickness of malaria, Lessing is calling attention to the fevers of these young people. There certainly follows a sick scene with more than one sick joke, in which Jimmy challenges Paul and stares him out.

After Paul killed one lone pigeon and they were waiting for more to come in sight, Jimmy became engrossed in the ways of a certain ant-eater. Here Lessing achieves one of her brilliant collages. We are conscious of two sets of actions taking place at the same time. Though the two engagements seem to be independent there emerges a coalescence that triggers the reader's mind off into his own private aesthetic and philosophical speculations. Jimmy poked around with a grass stem into the sand which, falling in miniature avalanches, destroyed "the exquisitely regular pit" made by the ant-eater. Paul grabbed the stem from Jimmy and fished out the tiny eater from the mass of heaving sand. Jimmy said nothing. Meanwhile (this word reminds us of Homer's and Virgil's technique of simultaneous action), Willi was reading. At the same time, Maryrose rested on her back and two more pigeons, which had flown into nearby trees, cooed. Paul shot them. Jimmy, hearing Paul give a soft call, retrieved the dead birds and went back to observing his ant-eater.

Meanwhile the dead birds were beginning to go bad. There was a smell of blood. Another bird appeared, and when Paul shot it, it fell to his feet. "It was still alive. It hung limp, but its black eyes watched us steadily" (reminiscent of the kicked pigeon on the London street). Paul made a sick joke: "Do you expect me to kill the thing in cold blood?" "'Yes,' said Jimmy...challenging him."

Death was mirrored on a smaller scale when "a very tiny ant, as light as a bit of fluff, had fallen over the edge of a pit and was at this moment bent double in the jaws of the monster." The ant in the jaws of the monster and the pigeon in the hands of Paul! Paul was also to die instantly (no harm in instant death). The **irony**, however, rests in the fact that Paul was to be killed by a thing, a machine, and by accident, not in the nature of things.

Meanwhile, a group of black farm-laborers passed by. They had been laughing and talking until they saw the vacationers. Then they became "silent, and went past with averted faces." It was as though they were trying to avoid the possibility of evil emanating from the whites.

This by-play caused Paul to discourse on the absurdity of the black and white impasse and from this on to the principles of destruction and happiness. Meanwhile another pigeon. Paul shot it and, since Jimmy didn't move, Paul had to serve as his own retriever. Maryrose's suspicion that she was going to be sick led Paul to another set of ironies. He recalled the good old days of African tribesmen. "Simple people killing each other for good reasons, land, women, food.... Not like us at all." Then he predicted that in fifty years all the black workers would be well clothed and well housed in semi-detached homes. "I shall fly out from England to inspect my overseas investments and per-adventure I shall fly over this area...." When more pigeons appeared, Paul shot two. Jimmy retrieved them and cried, "Seven. For God's sake, isn't that enough?" A small beetle attracted his attention. This new arrival was attacked by a large ant-eater, almost his equal in size. A ferocious fight ensued, until both were dead. "The moral is," said Paul, "that none but natural enemies should engage." Meanwhile Paul shot another bird, the last, at Maryrose's insistence. As though he were quitting because of his own decision, he remarked that more would have been an anticlimax.

## THE NOVELIST'S COMMITMENT

In the black notebook, Anna made some observations about Thomas Mann, a novelist who certainly had influenced her. She saw him as a writer of the old school who felt that his fiction should also be used as a vehicle for exploring not merely life as he saw it at certain times in certain places, but for explaining life in general in its widest philosophical sense. Still writing in her black book, she regretted that so much new fiction was merely the reporting of life for the sake of information. The reader must learn how life is lived in all the strange exciting places of the earth, where the action is. She deplored that writing was so often front-page journalism from which any commitment to explaining the reasons behind the deed had vanished.

Lessing's philosophy, Anna serving as amanuensis, is antinihilistic. She gets angry with those who despair, with those who typically are willing to describe war but haven't the courage to think about it. Her own personal searching brought her to a conclusion that was fresh out of her own experience. Wars can start when a people feel ashamed. They feel ashamed as a result of their cynicism and nihilism. Dialectically, one can see going to war against Hitler, who wanted to protect the superior German people from inferiors, as a consequence the British feeling guilty because they, the superiors, had overpowered the inferior dark natives of the colonies. Although this conclusion may seem a bit stretched, one can at least get from it a better understanding why some nations have said that the U.S. fought the yellow men in South East Asia because of an unwillingness to fight for the black citizens at home. War, according to Anna's thesis, can do a great deal of damage to non-combatants as well as the military. War is a refusal to put conflicting forces together and this refusal means impoverishment for everyone. There are no winners. This generality is particularized in Ted who looked upon his airforce experience as a mockery. He alternated between guilt feelings and impotent cynicism. Later he said that this was the time in his life of which he was most ashamed. Anna, as a person, was against anti-feeling; as a novelist, against anti-humanism. When she referred to the "evaporation of personality" she may have had in mind such novelists as Robbe-Grillet, Sartre, or Beckett. She combats their claim that a novelist has little right to be omniscient about a person's inner feelings as assumed from their smiles, their grimaces, their stance or shrugs. She contends she must remember a smile just as she must remember the hot African sun when it's cold and wet and dreary in London. If a smile or its absence helps a reader to feel the presence of Maryrose or Willi, she insists on describing it, willy-nilly.

## POLITICS AND SOCIAL SETTING

The group, no matter how informed its members were in the techniques of revolutionary movements, failed in their commitment to the blacks of Zambesia (the fictional name given by Lessing for the area south of the Zambesi river where she locates her story). These young people were too far ahead of the thinking of their British colonial contemporaries. The blacks were still too shocked by the white invasion to operate. Yet in retrospect, Anna, who by the time of her writing the black notebook had already been disillusioned by the Communist line and lingo, was pleased to see some success that grew out of their youthful dedication. Using one of her finest **metaphors** she wrote, "A dedicated faith in humanity spreads ripples in all directions."

By the time of making these notes, Anna had suffered another disillusionment. Having left Africa and endured some close penny-pinching before *The Frontiers of War* became a success, she had occasion to observe some segments of the British social system. She had not realized they were so rigidly defined.

It was only then that she could write about her Oxford-taught student pilot, Ted, "as a man who had understood from the beginning that there was one law for the rich and one for the poor." She could also write about Stanley (Ted's protege) that he was a trade unionist "tough, controlled, efficient, unscrupulous.... I never saw Stanley out of a shrewd control of himself, used as a weapon to get everything out of a world he took for granted was organized for the profit of others." Just as frightening was Paul whose monied ancestral pride maintained that (except when he was trying very deliberately to be witty) the British class system was beneficial all around.

Anna was equally angry at the American woman agent who suggested turning *The Frontiers of War* into a musical. It never occurred to this know-it-all that a white flier could never meet a black girl at a party...in Zambesia. Yet Anna was less angry at this woman when she saw the humor of her situation. Anna watched her woman-of-the-world mask crack wide open when she learned that Anna had once been a communist. The woman's provincialism forced Anna once more to the conclusion that anger is dishonest.

Anna was grateful for her African experiences and, inconsistently, for the cosmopolitanism of the upper-class British whom she learned to admire through Paul. Paul had once remarked to Jimmy that there was something about Africa that had marked him for life. His sheltered English upbringing had been better for his introduction "into the realities of nature in beak and claw." But Anna also remembered that Jimmy had been sadly cynical in his response. He had accused Paul of mouthing high-falutin' commonplaces. Africa had merely educated them in the "long bitterness of life." Lessing is enough of a realist to understand Jimmy's hatred of Africa which is mixed up with his fear of flying. There is truth in Jimmy's recognition "for the long bitterness of life."

## TRUTH AND FICTION

"How do I know that what I 'remember' was important?" Was Mrs. Boothby an "aborigine" or a lonely pathetic figure? Could she be both? Was George Hounslow the epitome of virility or sloppy sentimentality? Could he be both? Such problems lead Anna to introspection. Had she been honest in living with Willi and later dishonest when she had refused George? Challenging herself, can she go on to a sweeping inquiry? Is it true (and this is one of the novel's main theses and leads us into the Red Notebook) that every woman believes that if her man does not satisfy her, she has a right to go to another?

# THE GOLDEN NOTEBOOK

## THE RED NOTEBOOK

. . . . . . . . . . . . . . . . . . . . . . . . . . . . . . . . . . . . . . . . . . . . . . . . . . . . . . . . .

### VERBAL INCONTINENCE

This expression was used by Anna to describe a disease that seemed rampant among British Communists during the 1950s. There was so much talk that she felt she didn't want to add to it - not even by writing down her opinions in a diary. Instead, she took what was available, mostly from the press, and pasted clippings into her notebook. These clippings became a record of the frightful violence shaking so much of the world. Anna searched herself for the reasons why she had become a Communist and why she had stayed in the party after she was disillusioned by the talk-talk. She had joined out of disgust with the London literary world. She also felt that Communism was going to protect her from violence and at the same time recognized in herself a need "to protect an organization that people throw stones at."

The leader of the group who first interviewed her seemed suspicious of her as an intellectual. His experience showed that intellectuals drift in and out of the party. When he so categorized her, she was angry but rose to the criticism by answering, "If I were a raw recruit, I might be disillusioned by your attitude." He was shrewd enough to counter that he wouldn't have made the comment if he had not known she was an old hand. So she had signed up.

It was not long after that she began to realize that the only frank discussions she had about politics were with those who had already left the party. It was irritating to her to hear one of the Communists verbalize a Defense of the Soviet Union and still more irritating when she caught herself as having two personalities - her former open self and a Party fanatic. She seemed to be indulging in a private myth that she was biding her time until somehow the Soviets would return to true socialism. So she continued to carry her card. She still had ideals for a "better world" and deliberately deceived herself that Communism was still the answer.

## TRUTH AND DESPAIR

When Stalin died, Anna and Molly were upset. "We are being inconsistent, we ought to be pleased. We've been saying for months he ought to be dead." Molly took the attitude that they were upset because things can get worse, what we know about is less threatening. She foresaw an age of tyranny and continued terror. Anna's thinking went deeper and surfaced with the generalization that all men need heroes. The young Communists of London had made a great man out of Stalin regardless of the facts they had before them. She talked this over with Michael, who said, to her surprise, that perhaps Stalin was indeed great. "It might be true, mightn't it?... there's never any way of really knowing the truth about anything."

Later in 1954, when Molly was worried about the disappearance (in Czechoslovakia) of some friends, she went to Communist headquarters where she hoped to get more information. Instead, she received a lecture on the subject of capitalist lies. She exploded, "...you've got to learn to tell the truth and stop all this hole-and-corner conspiracy and telling lies about things."

When Anna started the Red Notebook and was pasting it up with political clippings, Michael was her lover. Anna and Michael needed each other at the time of their ever-increasing disillusionment with the world they once thought they could make into a better place. She tells the story of the night when they had received word that three of his friends had been hanged in Prague. He explained that it was impossible for these men to be traitors to Communism and impossible that the Party should frame and hang innocents. When Anna began talking about leaving the Party, he scolded her. Many people had left the Party because they felt they were leaving behind "murder, cynicism, horror, betrayal." She had expected a different reaction from Michael. She had supposed he would be sorry she was giving up. "Perhaps I'm with you, Anna, because it's nice to be with someone full of faith, even though one hasn't got it oneself."

## DIALOGUE AND STYLE

One becomes increasingly aware of the large amount of dialogue in *The Golden Notebook*. The realization, however, that the dialogue consists only rarely of small talk comes slower. There used to be a theory about writing fiction that if a novelist describes a conversation rather than presenting it, he thereby eliminates its chit-chat quality. Lessing, on the contrary, presents the conversation as conversation but without the chit-chat. As a result, her dialogues are not tape-recordings. She has developed the art of making her characters speak intelligently, meaningfully, and very often, wittily. The intensity of their speech contributes to its success, sometimes, it must be admitted, at the expense of what is called "good" grammar. It has been said that when Lessing races on, she shows herself to be the angry young woman.

Her occasional assassination of language, as we have pointed out, often makes compulsive reading - "The point is..." is an indication of her urgency. Doris Lessing seems to be thinking in words which force the reader to think - to fill in for himself - so that her "grammar" no longer annoys. When the content of what she wants to say has changed, demanding thereby a change in form, there are no egregious errors. She knows the rules and breaks them only on demand. She goes through many changes of pace. Her diversity of style has to be recognized as an achievement. Style even justifies her repetitions. The reader is unaware of her "again-saying" because what "the point is" is illustrated by a different set of circumstances in a new setting.

## ONE TALE TWICE-TOLD

Anna points out that a certain story she received in the mail could be read "as **parody, irony**, or seriously." The fact that this can be done she ascribes to "the thinning of language against the density of our experience." Briefly, the story that she reads aloud at a Party meeting, concerns Comrade Ted, young teacher who was invited to join a group going to Moscow. Arriving late at night, Ted sat down in his hotel room in order to go over his notes so that he could be thoroughly prepared for the events of the visit. Suddenly, two Comrades appeared who escorted him in the wee hours to the Kremlin where he was left alone with another hard-working Communist who turned out to be Stalin himself. The great man wanted to know all about the

English Communist Party. Sipping tea, Ted listened for hours until finally, Stalin begged forgiveness for detaining the teacher. After having explained that he had much work to do before the sun rose, he said goodbye to the Englishman who recalls: "We exchanged a wordless smile. I know my eyes were full-I shall be proud of these tears till I die! As I left, Stalin was refilling his pipe, his eyes already on a great pile of papers that awaited his perusal. I went out...after the greatest moment of my life." When Anna finished reading this obvious swill, one of the group remembered a story he had read in translation from the Russian. It told of two young men whose tractor had broken down in Red Square. They were trying unsuccessfully to fix it when a "burly figure" approached and asked what the trouble was. He looked and then pointed with the stem of his pipe at a certain part of the machinery. "Have you thought of that?" The young men followed the suggestion, the tractor roared into life. When they turned to thank the stranger who had been standing watching them with a fatherly twinkle in his eyes, they realized it was Stalin. The group had to laugh and the meeting broke up. Everyone felt hostile to everyone else and everyone knew it. The point was...

## DREAMS IN LITERATURE

Doris Lessing uses dream sequences sparingly in *The Golden Notebook*. Her interest in them had already been awakened but her scientific understanding of dreams seems still tentative. Later, in writing the last of *The Children of Violence* series, which as had been said she interrupted to produce The *Golden Notebook*, she utilizes dreams with broader implications.

As a literary device the dream has played many roles in literature. Homer used them, sometimes as thin veilings to describe a visitation from the gods. "And Aphrodite visited him in a dream." In Hebraic literature we witness the development of Joseph as a dreamer. When Joseph, the boy, dreamed of the grain bowing down to him, he took it to mean that his brothers must bow down. Instead, as we know, they threw him in the well and sold him to the Egyptians. Later, Joseph interpreted the Pharoah's dream of seven fat and seven lean years as prophetic. Students of psychology, having disallowed oneiromancy (divination by means of dreams), nevertheless recognize the value of Freud's dream analyses.

Today people can be taught to remember their dreams. Many who want to remember a dream will scribble something down in the dark so that, come morning, they can recapture what transpired in the dream world. Dreams often lead to creativity. Such dreams, we are told, are not related to day-dreams or what is scorned as idle imagination. On the other hand, psychiatrists have not written off day-dreaming as instruments of memory which can lead them to the truth about a personality.

Some story-telling novelists have dreamed up dreams for the sake of structure, plot, or character development, but anyone who has been fascinated by his own dreams can recognize a real dream from a fake. Sometimes an author will use both varieties. In a 1962 *New York Times* book review of *The Golden Notebook*, which was one of the most complimentary and discerning of all the American notices, attention was called to Lessing's use of "dreams and their cross-pollination of reality."

## THE RED DREAM

The "red dream" in the red notebook deserves close attention. Anna wanted to wake Michael but she knew with uncanny certainty she never would be able to describe the sensation of her dream. She wanted to catch the dream's meaning but this too was gone. All that remained was a feeling of elation. Instead of waking Michael to talk she cradled him in her arms. Suddenly politics, philosophy, art were unimportant. The truth was happiness.

The question that comes immediately to mind is, Does Anna begin kidding herself the moment she wakes up?

How long can such happiness last? The reader already knows that Michael is going to leave her - but the reader is already getting a hint that Anna's love for Michael is never to vanish as had vanished her feelings for men she had known earlier.

Very soon afterward Anna tried to be scientific and objective, even hard. In this connection it is noteworthy that she made no mention during the dream or at her awakening of the possible occurrence of menstruation. The avoidance of the subject at this point in the red book almost calls attention to it. In another passage Lessing, when she has another purpose in mind, is far less elusive.

## POST RED

Anna left the Party in 1954. From there on out the notebook consists mostly of pastings and clippings, with only a few notations in her own handwriting. She had reacted against her activism. She chided herself for wasting weeks and months in work for the Party which accomplished nothing. In one outstanding passage she remembered her pointless discussions with the comrades as meaningless attempts to reason with them. Putting the words into the mouth of a visitor she says: "It is as if you proposed to appeal to a professional burglar to retire because his efficiency was giving his profession a bad name."

Her last entry in the book is a small short story in itself. It mirrors in a distorted and cynical way her happy red dream. It concerns Harry, ex-teacher, who had not simply left the Party but had been expelled. Because he was a war cripple (fighting in Spain) he could not take part in World War II. He lived like a Spartan performing heroic deeds, rescuing people from bombs and burning buildings. He had become legendary: the ubiquitous limping savior who could vanish when it came time to praise. There was another side to Harry; he collected books and clippings about the Soviet Union. The war ended and his heroism turned to rescuing poor children, not from bomb craters but from ignorance. Less dramatic was a widow with youngsters who fell in love with him: they all moved into his one room. Meanwhile, he studied Russian, and learned the inside history of Russia, its intrigues, its blood baths. He kept preparing for the day when the Communists would see the light and his "history" would be invaluable. Harry thought his day had truly come when an old friend and comrade had him placed on a delegation to Moscow. Harry could not conceive that he was being invited for mere friendship's sake. The Soviets, perhaps even Khrushchev himself, wanted to learn what he, Harry, knew about their history. When in Moscow he learned the truth. His world collapsed. Hysterical, he spent the night lecturing not a high official but an exhausted tour guide, who was too polite to shut him up. She worried about his being a little mad, especially when he suspected she might have him locked up - sent to Siberia. But Harry returned to England and when we last hear about him he was ill-looking but strangely thankful for his Moscow visit. He married the widow who was pregnant again. So ends the red notebook. What has it proved? Anything? That blood proves nothing?

# THE GOLDEN NOTEBOOK

## THE YELLOW NOTEBOOK

### CONTINUITY

Lessing deliberately uses the same names for different figures in the various notebooks. We learn more about the one from the namesake. The grown Michael is explained by the portrait of the child Michael and the child is the creation of the woman who was mystified by the adult. Paul Tanner has Paul's name and has many of the airman's characteristics. But Paul Tanner looks like Jimmy and his background resembles Ted's. He fights to get ahead, to rise above his class by means of education and a succession of scholarships. His compassion for the poor (Ted's) blocks him in his ambition (Paul's). He is a sensualist like George Hounslow without Hounslow's courage.

The characters in the yellow notebook who closely resemble those in the red are more striking in their similarities when their names undergo a change. Ella is quite close to Anna, who remains in the yellow notebook as Ella's creator. Ella has Julia as her friend as Anna had Molly. Julia and Molly are nearly indistinguishable. Jack is another Willi, matured since Mashopi days. We recognize Willi in Ella's description of Jack "as the efficient type of lover - the man who is not sensual, has learned lovemaking out of a book, probably called How to Satisfy Your Wife." Patricia Brent is a continuity within a continuity. She is Ella's symbol of herself projected as an older woman and Ella emerges for the older woman as a recreation of her youth. This may sound complicated but the events of the story bring understanding as well as recognition.

Remember the grasshoppers? At Mashopi? Consider the passage where Ella's father was annoyed that his reading had been interrupted by her curiosity concerning his wife, her mother. Here are the exact words: "The book slowly lowers to her father's lean and stick-like thighs. The yellowish dry lean face was flushed, and the blue eyes were protuberant, like an insect's." He is an old, old grasshopper. Sex no longer matters to him, though God does. The next world is important because in this one the myriads of human bugs are merely messy masses. "People are just cannibals unless they leave each other alone." Then another insecticide reference: "People don't help each other, they are better apart."

## PERSONALITY REVEALED

Whereas Paul is Paul and Jimmy and Ted and George Hounslow, all four rolled into one, Ella in her part is not a mixture but a mixed up person, a circus mirror image of Anna.

We have been shown Ella as a mistress, free and bound at the same time and also as a wife both recollected and projected. Then finally we see her in Paris after the curtain has been rung down on both her erstwhile selves.

Paris, "animated with greening trees and strolling people." Having dinner alone in such a setting would have been, five years earlier, a pleasant occasion. What possibilities for an encounter! Instead, Ella went back to her hotel to bed and masturbation, kidding herself about her former selves.

Realizing the yellow cowardice within the present state of her make-up, she determined to surmount it and decided upon a course of flirtation with the French editor whose magazine had been her excuse for coming to the capital. "Monsieur Brun (the name itself testifies to Lessing's humor), a large well-kept, ox-like (animal symbolism) young man who greeted her with an excess of good manners - a species of highly trained middleclass animal."

Ella prepared to make use of him but alas "the great well-groomed ox" was engaged to be married. His intended joined them at lunch during which it became evident that their marriage was to be a well managed arrangement, inevitably to include at exactly the proper times, a small child, perhaps a nurse, and then, of course, a mistress. Ella foresaw it all with clarity and yet in her imagined, vividly projected use of the vivacious Frenchman, she had been, she was forced to admit, no better than the frightened future wife. Such a fraud she had become.

## WOMEN AGAINST MEN

Ella could not imagine a life without a man. When she let Paul make love to her in the field because she had been immediately stirred by his acquaintance, he teased her that she had planned the happening which she denied, of course. Of this he later reminded her, again and again. It was important to his ego.

He wanted to feel that it was she who had started their life together. Better to forget that he had tucked a soft rug in the car that first afternoon just in case.

Before he took her naked in the field, in broad daylight, he had talked almost nonchalantly as a smart psychiatrist would, about her husband - and he had told her at some length about his wife. He had taken his time with his build-up so that she could later say "our bodies understood each other."

In this scene, and there are several such, some to be sure less romantic, there is never any mention of contraception. (It was still 1959.) Such an omission is a weakness in notebook records as frank as these - unless we deliberately recall that the "yellow" book is in itself a symbol of weakness, cowardice.

When Ella had finished her novel and it had been accepted for publication, Paul made fun of it. "We men might just as well resign from life." Then he continued seriously, "My dear Ella, don't you know what the great revolution of our time is? The Russian revolution, the Chinese revolution - they're nothing at all. The real revolution is women against men." He accused women for not having faith in what they were. Answering, she implied that the reason for the revolution was that men were getting madder and madder and women saner and saner. "Sex, the difficulty of writing about sex for women, is sex is best when not thought about, not analyzed. Women deliberately choose not to think about technical sex. They get irritable when men talk technically, it's out of self-preservation. They want to preserve the spontaneous emotion that is essential for their satisfaction." A very sane comment on one level; emotional on another.

Anna analyzed how she wrote about Ella whom she had created as a creator. Anna could be clinical at the same time she was saying that Ella, the character, refused to be. When Anna became "technical" on the subject of the penis, the clitoris, orgasm, manipulation, we have to forget that Anna is a character too. We don't realize that Lessing is involving us in the novelistic structural device of Anna/Ella.

The concept is a witness also to Mrs. Lessing's art. Her sensitivity comes into play. She can also turn prudery into comedy. A fine example of this is in the famous, or infamous, scene concerning the venerable professor's lecture on the sex life of the swan.

## COMPLEX OF EMOTIONS

Lessing's highly perceptive insight in the complexity of human emotions is again revealed when Ella and Paul first met and were obviously attracted to each other. Ella was aware that his pride (sexual) would be wounded if she did not respond. This made her feel like escaping because (even if she didn't know it) she was suddenly and forcibly reminded that in years gone by she had dishonestly forced herself to respond when she had married her husband not out of love but out of exhaustion. His courtship had been so violently persistent. She had felt suffocated.

She didn't want a repetition of such dishonesty with Paul. Her mind uncontrollably jumped back to her husband's attempt toward the end of their distraught union to win her by going off with another woman. Enough jealousy was to be produced to overwhelm Ella. Instead Ella had been merely relieved and then glad when he was free to marry her stand-in.

Ella's reactions were never simple. She was always too sensitive to the other partner. On occasions when she had been with a married man to whose unknown wife she had been unconsciously feeling superior, she had become depressed. She felt a guilt which she tried to pass off or at least justify. It is "not my guilt, it is the guilt from the past, it has to do with the double standard which I repudiate." She turned to ice when she heard a claim that he always took pains that his wife, who was a "good girl," never suspected him when he went "off the rails."

Her resentment grew even deeper, perhaps inconsistently so, when she whispered to herself that "his wife, the woman who is waiting for him miles away somewhere across London will know, the moment he enters the bedroom, that he has been sleeping with another woman, from his self-satisfied jauntiness." How clearly we know Ella was a wife!

In another complicated incident (quite a list of them is possible) Ella seems to be what would really shock her - a petulant little girl, anything but a "free woman." In recording Ella's fretful, unmouthed conversation (what academics label as interior monologues) Mrs. Lessing shows her own idiosyncratic skill.

For example, Ella murmuring to herself, defines a real man. "If he is a real man she (any woman) is, in a sense, put to sleep by him. She does not think about sex."

## MALE EGO

The point is, as Ella and Julia and Anna and Molly would say, they know very little of the male ego as it jogs through the yellow notebook.

The two women, cheerful and friendly with each other, make fun of men, particularly men who take pleasure in a fight. They take satisfaction in the victory of getting a woman into bed - sufficient unto the night. In sensing this, however, the two women forget their own callous satisfaction of being victorious over their lovers' wives, those unexciting, dull women.

It is a very self-righteous and perhaps self-deluded Julia who claimed she takes a men to bed at that moment when he "looks all wounded in his masculinity, one can't bear it, one needs to bolster him up."

On the other hand, it is true these two women came up against some genuine male egoists. There is Dr. West, "an altogether brisk, competent man" and the self-confident Paul who knew when to retreat rather than force love. Another example of male self-interest is unquestionably the editor who "had not one spark of that instinctive warmth for a woman, liking for a woman."

## INCOMPETENT WOMEN

According to her father, Ella's mother was an incompetent woman. This isolated man, who knew a lot about philosophy and religion, who had amassed amounts of secretly written poetry, communicated, according to his unsparing daughter, in "high inaudible squeaks." This ex-colonel answered her questions vaguely because of the vagueness of his private world.

His wife was "a good woman" but sex just wasn't any part of her. That the lack was his own fault never entered his head. "When I couldn't stick it, I went out and bought myself a woman. What did you expect?"

The last question seemed to be directed by the old man not at the daughter but at her dead mother. An old **cliche** comes to mind with a variation: "Like father, like daughter." It makes us wonder about Paul's comment, "There is no such thing as a frigid woman, there are only incompetent men." For the first time, Lessing seems to be suggesting in the yellow notes (always somewhat fraudulent and not infrequently comic) that there is no such animal as a frigid man; there are only incompetent women.

Putting triviality aside, Lessing proposes a keen distinction. Men can be incompetent in sex - women incompetent in love. Ella had her finest experiences with Paul. Deeply in love with him, she told herself that he would marry her. In this she believed she could trust him. She was incompetent in her self-delusion. Other women have foregone sex to test the love of a man - not to test their own love but to win their man as a lawful wedded husband. Ella's behavior did not confirm her desire for what other women achieve - marriage. It is a fact, learned too late by her, that when the hope of marriage withdrew further and further into the background, love became mechanical. The hope or fact of marriage would appear to be an ingredient in lovemaking. That Paul felt her deep love for him and knew she had marriage in mind but nevertheless walked out on her is proof of her incompetence in love.

## SISYPHUS MYTH

This archetypal **theme** has already been mentioned in connection with Lessing herself and her fight against mountainous stupidity. She offers a variation to the **theme** in her delineation of Paul, the doctor, the healer.

Paul says, "A poor man who is frightened of his landlord and the police is a slave." In Great Britain the upper classes know this but the working classes don't. He feels his job is to tell them because "great men are too great to be bothered." "We [he and Ella] spend our lives fighting to get people very slightly more stupid than ourselves to accept truths that the great men have always known...you and I are the boulder pushers...the boulder is the truth that the great men know by instinct, and the mountain is the stupidity of mankind."

Sincere and intelligent as his comment is, there lies beneath it a subtle **irony**. He is himself complacently dull and class conscious so when he substitutes the word instinct for upper class breeding, we excuse his apparent mistake because of his sympathy for the class he struggled to transcend. "I wish I had died, Ella." At this point the subject of death Ella was writing about in her novel becomes a living and life-giving theme. The Sisyphus figure has become a Christ figure. The roles of the boulder, the pusher, and the mountain change places. Mankind must be saved from stupidity - even if one man must be sacrificed in the attempt. A thesis, new to the yellow book notes, is hereby given birth. The subject is not stupidity but naivety. The nativity of naivety. In order to create, one must be naive, ingenuous, innately virtuous. Ella, lacking in these characteristics, had been locked in her own stupidity.

## MAN CREATES WOMAN

"Paul gave birth to Ella, the naive Ella and...he put her intelligence to sleep,...with her willing connivance, so...she floated darkly in her love for him, on her naivety,...another word for a spontaneous creative faith." For five years, living with her guilty and affectionate Paul, Ella enjoyed such a faith. When she lost it she could no longer create out of naivety but was forced to return to her writing as work to be somehow got through. She was forced to write, not out of naivety but out of sophistication. This is sad. Later on this judgment of sophistication develops into a major **theme**, when yellow and black and red and blue turn into golden.

## IRONY AND ANGER

Meanwhile, Ella, who doesn't think her novel will do anyone any good, keeps on writing about suicide and her yellow-bellied young man. "I'll just write it for myself." In deceiving herself as a do-gooder she is doing no good. After her visit to Paris, Ella decided that the cure for manlessness was work. Her new novel, while not perhaps a "creation," would at least be a record. She knew she could no longer write of her experience with Paul. As a subject she had to put it aside. She was no longer free in what she could put down on paper. She had, therefore, lost her independence. Because of love for him, she could not "go public." Therefore, what could be written for the public would inevitably be dishonest.

It was no good telling herself she ought to be more like a man - put her work first. All her woman's emotions, which struck her as being commonplace, are "still fitted for a kind of society that no longer exists." The free woman is nostalgic. As expected, her deceit, her dishonesty, grows into anger. Her anger nevertheless doesn't blind her realization of her own cowardice. This is the same woman who, frightened by the city of London, forced herself to walk through its mean districts. But Ella's walks accomplish more than dispersing her fear. She is always learning. She is sharp enough to observe that mean neighborhoods can change, almost accidentally. A certain painter (we shall meet him in another guise) took a wreck of a house in a run-down, once bombed, street and made it beautiful. Some canny professional people moved into the district and renovated more houses, but - and here Ella recognized the **irony** - these new people were so busy being professional and making money that they neglected their front gardens - the kind that had been tended in front of the old ruins. The discrepancy in values made her angry.

## MIDDLE-CLASS AND WORKING CLASS

Doris Lessing deplores the British class distinctions. As the daughter of a colonial in Zambesia where the distinctions were mostly made between white and black, the hierarchy of English classes disturbed her. Ella is created as a middle-class person whom no interest in liberal social concepts could change, just as Julia's education, sensitivity, intelligence, and sophistication could not lift her out of her working-class attitudes. At best, each woman could laugh at herself and her class. Julia's rough humor saved her and with it she was able to protect Ella.

Paul, who humorously called himself a "witch doctor," a label he knew he received from many of his lower-class patients, understood the problems of the lost souls whose letters to the magazine it was Ella's job to answer. Ella despaired that the good advice she tried to give was apt to be valueless. She felt somewhat cheap whereas Paul grew angry. He blamed the "old-fashioned doctors," the middle class-oriented medical establishment. Ella viewed his concern as a criticism of his class rather than of his profession. His anger was never directed at his patients but at their helplessness for which they were blameless. Ella understood all this because of her own experiences with factory girls during the war but she could never deliver a whitewash. A trace of contempt always remained, even with Paul. It could be said, perhaps with an unconscious snobbishness, of his voice, "a warm voice, a little rough where the edges of an uneducated accent remained." It is ironic that she failed to recognize that he was more formally educated than she had ever been.

We can see how corroding contempt can become by Ella's attitude toward Mrs. West who happens not to be working class but middle class. In this case her disdain is even more misplaced. Mrs. West is simply the wife of another man who had been attracted to Ella. When Ella sees her as a kind of middle-class person who can only tolerate those who are like their own, Ella is certainly a traitor to her class. She is not a "free woman" when she is scornful over Mrs. West and her "disinfecting phrases." This is indeed the yellow book of career girls and the lunatic fringe.

## UNSUCCESSFUL MARRIAGE

Ella had not remained in the marriage in which she had been compromised even though the husband's actions had been encouraged by her. Because her husband had married at once after the divorce, it was thought he had left her for another woman. In America the woman usually seeks the divorce to rid herself of an unfaithful husband. In England, even though the marital situation is the same, the husband seeks the divorce because it is considered unflattering to the woman when she cannot hold her man. Ella's own egoism and extreme repugnance toward her husband caused her to set little value on what others thought or might think. She is the reverse of Mrs. West who hung on to her husband in spite of his wanderings. At one point, even before she had cause with Ella in particular, Mrs. West deliberately let Ella know that her husband discussed his work with her. Thus her "wifely" rights were established.

Paul, coming home in the morning "to get a clean shirt," suggests that his wife doesn't mind living as she does. He says she could leave him if she wanted to. Nothing stops her from returning to her parents, but "she depends on me completely… it's how she likes to live."

Ella, who believes that no woman wants to live without love, is accused by him of being an idealist. "You," he said, "measure everything against some kind of ideal that exists in your head, and if it doesn't come up to your beautiful notions then you condemn it out of hand, or you pretend to yourself that it's beautiful even if it isn't…you say scornfully, Oh security! Oh respectability! But Muriel wouldn't. They're very important to her." Inconsistently, and with even more cynicism, Ella remarked on a different wave-length: "Love was a mirage and the property of woman's magazines."

## WORLD SICKNESS

"What sort of a doctor is it who sees his patients as symptoms of world sickness?" Paul asked Ella. Nobody cared about the lonely women who wrote to columnists like Ella. Ella agreed with him but when another's loneliness came close to home, she was forced to do some soul-searching. When Ella went to the home where her lover lived with his wife Muriel and their children, she was repelled by the alternation of semi-plushness, bad taste and shabbiness. She was jolted out of herself when she saw, on the kitchen table, dozens of copies of Women at Home, the very "nasty and snobbish" magazine she wrote for. She had no right to sneer at the women who read her stuff. She was the sick one? Hers was the sickness of "I'm no worse than anyone else" - an important **theme** with Lessing.

## PRIVATE SICKNESS

We have noted that Paul as a sensitive and self-made doctor and psychiatrist really cared for Ella's correspondents whom she knew she was deluding. His concern and hers for the "outside" others stood in the way of their own relationship. Attempts at being objective, being intelligent about their own anomalous situation, seemed almost flagellating. Why do they have to experiment? Is experimentation the only path to truth? "If you love a woman," Paul said, "sleeping with another woman means nothing." Ella, who had also been experimenting away from Paul, had a different reaction. She went a step further because it suddenly struck her that Paul's "sleeping away" meant that he was with his wife of thirteen years - hardly what one would call "experimenting." Their separate ways were dissimilar even though the conclusions were alike. When they both tested their responses with others, they found the others irrelevant.

After Paul had "ditched her," Ella's phrase to Julia, Ella's bitterness turned to anger. She went out, bought new clothes, had her hair restyled "in a soft provocative shape," left Julia's house, moved into a new flat where she found, after all, that she was merely waiting for Paul, night after night. "Being mad is not being able to stop yourself doing something that you know to be irrational."

We are made aware of a more disturbing sickness - that of the child, Ella's son Michael. The boy had loved his own father. Paul, the new man in the house, who had children of his own, was insensible to Ella's child. He failed to see (his error is compounded by the fact that he was a psychiatrist) that Michael needed masculine affection. Ella, who indeed recognized the deficiency, did nothing. She worried that Michael would never again have a "natural warm response" to a man. Just words to Ella but more than words to the reader. Lessing is asking two separate questions; first, Was the sophisticated "free" mother "unnatural"? and secondly, Would she be the cause of "unnaturalness"?

## ANOTHER NIGHTMARE

After Paul had left her, had in fact taken a post in Nigeria, Ella dreamed she was in Paul's wife's untidy house. She was merely waiting in the house to which Paul was sure to return. At first his wife's ghost was present and then it wasn't. The wife had gone to join Paul. She woke up screaming at her dreamt prophecy. She didn't know the nightmare would come true, a fact that has literary value. The oneiric aspects which Lessing has here incorporated shall be discussed fully under a later heading.

## SUICIDE

This is the main **theme** of the novel Ella was writing. Its **protagonist** didn't know he was going to kill himself until the moment he did it. He never realized he had been preparing for that moment. In making this point the novelist was to contrast the surface of life with the subconscious, underlying motif of death.

Paul once made fun of Ella. He accused her of being pretentious concerning suicide. She had not experienced what he could not escape knowing at first hand because of his working class origins and his being a doctor. Charging her of using him to get at his knowledge he, however, took pains to instruct her. She learned more on her own.

Climbing into the aircraft which had once already returned for repairs to the Paris airport, Ella, along with all the disquieted passengers, was forced to consider death. "For a mother to die in an air crash - that's sad, but it's not damaging. Not like a suicide. How odd - the phrase is, to give a child life, but a child gives life to its parent when the parent decides to live simply because to commit suicide would hurt the child."

What is really odd is her behavior the following night, her first at home, when she hurt her child by leaving him to go out with the large square American whom she had met on the plane. In hurting the child, she, in a sense, committed suicide. Her moment of truth was short-lived, burnt out like a fire-fly's.

Ella's father, "who might have been a poet or a mystic," also objected to Ella's novel about suicide. "That poor stick, what did he want to kill himself for?" To the old man, suicide was not a subject one wrote about. Ella, of course, disagreed, with persistence. She tried to explain that what she was actually writing about was the lack of happiness as a cause for suicide. Happiness was an essential ingredient in her thesis. Her father would not accept her contention. Happiness is something he claims he never thought about. That the world owes no one anything is refuted by her argument that he and his generation never demanded enough of the world. "We are prepared," she continues, "to experiment with ourselves, to try and be different kinds of people." To herself she went further. "I've got to accept the patterns of self-knowledge which mean unhappiness or at least a dryness. But I can twist it into victory. A man and a woman - yes. Both at the end of their tether. Both cracking up because of a deliberate attempt to transcend their own limits. And out of chaos, a new kind of strength."

Motifs And The Novelist's Craft. Ella's hero, who is a suicide, foreshadows Tommy's attempt in the "Free Women." Tommy is Molly's son whom we follow in those sections of the book where Anna is not a notebook-scribbler. These sections come before each set of the continuing notebook stories. Again, we point out, the notebook structure or device is used to illuminate a theme.

"If I were to write this novel," says Ella, via Anna, via Doris Lessing, "the main motif would be Paul's wife to whom he is unfaithful." When she, Ella, Anna or Mrs. Lessing remarks that Paul will not return to her, the reader is let in on a fact in advance. Suspense has been created. At this point the author transfers omniscience to the reader. He is told in advance what Ella gradually comes to understand. She "imagines" herself as a wife. She imagines herself without Paul and she becomes clinging "like a wife" to protect herself from hurt. The **irony** rests in the fact that she, thereby, causes her own loss. Going deeper, Mrs. Lessing raises a more universal question, how much does your imagination control your life?

The role that Paul plays is illustrative. He "imagines" himself as a "self-hating rake, free, casual, heartless." This is what Ella condemns as his "negative self." She analyzes with bitterness that his play-acting is a "mockery of the truth," which it is. Mrs. Lessing's sophisticated insight is rivaled only by the economy of her elucidation.

One cannot, Anna claims, write a story as analysis. A story must provide a feeling of life at a given moment. The moment has already evanesced when you analyze it as an event. When she says, "Literature is analysis after the event," we immediately think of William Wordsworth, the romantic poet. He called poetry "an emotion recollected in tranquility." Keats, another romantic who was born later (1795) but died sooner, equated beauty and truth. If one equates beauty, truth, poetry and literature, one becomes aware again of Mrs. Lessing's main inquiry into how the truth is to be told.

## THE AMERICAN IS MORE ATTRACTIVE

Is it the truth that Lessing dislikes Americans? Is her broad-brush description evidence of a deep-seated aversion? Is the fast-moving vignette in the middle of the yellow book a haughty travesty? Brought forth almost entirely in dialogue, it is both funny and convincing - Yeah - that guy - the hick - the healthy savage - Hell - Boy, Oh Boy - such fun in the sack - man!

The oaf of an American who can take'em or leave 'em would appear to come out on top whereas Ella is shown close to her worst. Cy, who could make almost twenty telephone calls in thirty minutes, who was so busy getting ahead, being a big-name doctor with international connections, with ambitions to become a senator from his home state, could with bravado but sincere and old-fashioned humility, invite Ella to dinner. He could order the biggest steak they had in the place. He could obtain the best bottle of wine for Ella when she asked for it and could, without embarrassment, drink coca-cola himself. He repelled her physically and it upset her, when, still at dinner, he laid his large white hand on her arm, making "her breasts lift and sting," "Her thighs were wet...the discovery that she wanted to be in bed with him split her."

This man from the west who had married "the prettiest and classiest girl" felt just fine. He was perfectly honest with himself and with Ella, but didn't know quite how to behave with the sophisticated woman she had decided to be. She, with characteristic self-assurance, took control of the situation.

If later she suffered a "physical disappointment," she could not honestly blame him. Nevertheless she did. She was honestly annoyed but dishonest when she said: "I could no more understand a woman like your wife than fly." In the same vein, there is no question of his sincerity when he replies "No, I don't think you could at that."

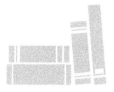

# THE GOLDEN NOTEBOOK

## THE BLUE NOTEBOOK

. . . . . . . . . . . . . . . . . . . . . . . . . . . . . . . . . . . . . . . . . . . . . . . . . . .

### PSYCHO-ANALYSIS

Even though Anna told Mother Sugar that she had not come to her because she had a writer's block but because she kept having experiences that failed to touch her, the analyst asked, "Why don't you write another book... So you don't believe in art... So?" What were her dreams? She had so many one wonders how many she made up for Mother Sugar's benefit. In her dreams she had a fear of being frigid, of having no feelings. In real life she seemed to stare at herself as though she were at a movie. "Play, mummy," said her child when she watched her mother insensibly move a block or two. She seemed frozen and complained to Mother Sugar that the only reality seemed to be the death and destruction that went on in the world. Once she had joined the Communists because they seemed to be the only people who cared. Then she didn't care about them any longer. She was merely "fond" of her friend Molly. She enjoyed sleeping with Michael but he might run out on her. She laughed when Mother Sugar scolded her. This was at the beginning of her sessions with the one she was soon to call "the most intelligent wise old woman."

The blue diary reports another scene with Mother Sugar that obviously replays a situation in the Ella and Paul story. Anna had told the analyst that she became frigid on the very night Michael had warned her that he did not intend to marry her. At this confession Mother Sugar told Anna about a woman who had been frigid for three years with a man she loved deeply and never had an orgasm until the day they were legally married. "What a pillar of reaction you are," said Anna and laughed but the point the experienced psychiatrist was making was no laughing matter for Mrs. Lessing's fencing with the blue and black notebooks.

After having several dreams that Michael would leave her, Anna grumbled to Mother Sugar. Instead of being much alive in her dreams and half-dead awake, Anna changed to being very sensitive awake and unmoved asleep. Thereupon Mother Sugar asked her if she had to say but one thing that she had received from her sessions what would Anna's answer be. Her surprising reply was that Mother Sugar had taught her to cry; also that she was "a hundred times more vulnerable." To this Mother Sugar said with emphasis, "You are very much stronger."

## MORE DREAMS

Anna had a repetitive dream which she called the bad dream. In it she was menaced in one way or another. Her attacker appeared in the shape of an inhuman dwarf. In it Mother Sugar also appeared very large and powerful (in life she was anything but), like a friendly witch. The analyst heard the dream out and said to Anna, "When you are on your own, and you are threatened, you must summon the good witch to your aid." "You," said Anna. Mother Sugar answered, "No, You, embodied in what you have made of me." It was as though Mother Sugar were handing her a "flowering branch or, perhaps, a talisman against evil." The experience of contact with this woman didn't end with the sessions. As we shall see, the yeast went on working.

In Anna's dreams are found still other examples of Doris Lessing's animal symbolism. Anna dreamt that a group of businessmen at the end of a museum-like hall were waiting for her to turn over to them a miniature casket. When they handed over large sums of money for it and she opened it, she saw, not a beautiful object but a mass of ugly fragments from wars around the world, including nasty bits of flesh. She quickly passed it over but when the men in their turn opened it, they seemed delighted with what they saw. She didn't wish to look but finally she got a glimpse of what was in it. It was a crocodile, not an image of one in jade or emerald but alive "for large frozen tears rolled down its cheeks and turned to diamonds." Believing she had cheated the business people, she laughed aloud and woke up. Later she identified the museum hall as Mother Sugar's room, a shrine to art where she had so many half-hours. Still later when seeing herself mirrored in a shop window, Anna recognized the wry face she was wearing "as the grin on the snout of that malicious little green crocodile in the crystal casket" of her dream. The reptilian symbol, reminiscent of the Garden of Eden, is a warning to Anna.

## INTELLECTUAL TEARS

"All I can remember when I wake is that I have been crying." William Blake, way back in the eighteenth century, called the tear "an intellectual thing." The earthier Mother Sugar explained from the same viewpoint but in different words, "The tears we shed in our sleep are the only genuine tears we shed in our lives - the waking tears are self-pity." Sometimes Anna went to sleep knowing she was going to cry and that pleased her, masochistically. Mother Sugar, without mentioning the ancient Greek playwrights, repeated that there is pleasure in pain. It is a nostalgic pain that makes one cry. It is nostalgia for a former time in life. Anna's African childhood had made her write her book which, in spite of its success, had not taken away what she now realized was its poison. She had known it all along. "All self-knowledge is knowing, on deeper and deeper levels, what one knew before."

Anna's friend Molly cried, if not less intellectually, certainly more personally. With "her hands lying on her knees; they look limp and discouraged" (Mrs. Lessing always has this actress talk with her body), Molly says "What frightens me is, I never seem to be able to see anything pure in what people do - do you know what I mean?... I find myself getting all cynical and psychological about it..." These are the I, I, I tears of a self-pitying free woman!

## DIARY-WRITING AS TECHNIQUE

Diary-writing as part of a novel is almost as old a fictional device as the love letter. Mrs. Lessing has given autobiographical writing a new twist. She has devised a diary within a diary. Mother Sugar told Anna that writing a diary is the beginning of what she thinks of as "unfreezing."

Certainly many authors have kept notebooks or diaries, Henry James, for example. Anna cut out newspaper accounts and carefully pasted them into her blue notebook - the "fact" notebook. The blue book contained four years' accumulation of such clippings before she once again turned to presenting the news in her own summations. How true her collage of current events was is subject to question when one notices the sources - *The Express, Daily Telegraph, New Statesman,*

*Los Angeles Times.* These papers might be "true" from the liberal's viewpoint but "biased" from a conservative's.

President Harry Truman was urged to drop an atom bomb on North Korea. Prime Minister Atlee postponed social services in order to spend pounds 100 million more on Defense. The U.S. was in grave danger, created by Soviet leaders. Troops used tear gas. "A man alive in 1951 and a woman alive in 2051 might be matched in 2251 to produce a child by a pre-natal foster mother." McCarthy's witch hunts produced a low-type of conformity, "a new orthodoxy from which a man dissents at his economic peril." Airforce Colonel Robert Scott, on the signing of a preliminary treaty with Germany in October 1952, hoped that the U.S. and Germany would "stand shoulder to shoulder to resist the threat of Communism." He hoped and prayed that someday his Air Base would be manned by a German Wing Commander with a new Luftwaffe. And on the 8th of May 1953, America discussed United Nations action "to curb Communist aggression in S.E. Asia" and deployed large quantities of planes and ammunition to Indo-China.

Such notes about the early fifties set the novel in time, but when included by Mrs. Lessing in 1962 they jangle the readers' nerves with irony. Reading them in 1973, the **irony** becomes the more horrifying.

## WRITING AS ART

Since our chief **protagonist** is a novelist who has "dried up" after hitting the best-seller lists, we can expect a certain amount of comment concerning aesthetics. What little theorizing is included in *The Golden Notebook* bursts forth in small doses. It is never obscure or pretentious.

Anna carried on her job with the Communist publishing house not merely out of political and social convictions where she might gain reinforcement or spot new Communist trends. She endured it because she was tantalized by the possibility that in reading so much "bad, dead, banal writing" she might by chance come upon a "paragraph, a sentence, a phrase, of truth." She is forced "to acknowledge that the flashes of genuine art are all out of deep, suddenly stark, undisguisable private emotion. Even in translation there is no mistaking these lightning flashes of genuine personal feeling. And I read this dead stuff praying that just once there may be a short story, a novel, even an article," written wholly from genuine personal feeling.

Is it a paradox that this last quotation is itself an example of bad writing? The word flashes is repeated twice, once accompanied to make the **cliche** lightning flashes. The word genuine is used three times, twice in the phrase genuine personal feeling which is still another **cliche**. And grammatically we have a fault in the dangling participle praying. Dead stuff doesn't pray.

Didn't Mrs. Lessing know what she was doing? Or did she in the heat of her own flash keep the ink spurting? Was there no time to change a phrase? The rules be damned! The urgency of the words, the medium in this case, becomes at least a vital part of the message. As was pointed out in connection with the yellow notebook, there is emotion in feeling and feeling in emotion.

Feelings, as Plato declared so long ago in his *Philebus*, are a mixture of pleasure and displeasure, pleasure seldom, if ever, free of displeasure. Pleasure and displeasure create tension and true feeling is tension. The urgency of Lessing's words in the above passage, pleasingly or displeasingly, written, creates tension and is, by extension, art. This passage, even if one goes so far as to condemn its stylistic idiosyncrasies, may be considered art. Students in making their own evaluations should be aware of the differences between style and art. A conscious artist never takes shelter in conformity. This would be sterility. Part of Lessing's power, for better not for worse, lies in her non-conformity. Her work gains in its universal or artistic character because it is unique, not typical. Art begins where conformity leaves off. We must remember, even in our personal embroilment in the action story, that *The Golden Notebook* is a novel about a writer and her writings.

## SKIP THE NEWSPAPERS

When Anna admitted that her clippings had all been of war, murder, chaos, and misery, Mother Sugar pointed out that Anna had been making her news selections into instructions on how to dream the nightmares she reported. The frustrating events dried up her feelings and kept her from writing. "Why can't you understand," asked Anna, "that I can't pick up a newspaper without what's in it seeming so overwhelmingly terrible that nothing I could write would seem to have any point at all?"

"Then you shouldn't read the newspapers." But Anna was no ostrich. And neither is Mrs. Lessing, as is evident from her more recent novel *The Four-Gated City*.

## DISCONTINUITY

We have been reading about Willi, Max, two Michaels, two Pauls, one Saul and a variety of lesser men. Because it isn't always easy to keep them straight, we can suspect Anna and Molly had been having too many "What's wrong-with-men sessions."

The blue notebook repeats that Willi and Max are obviously two portraits of the same man. The Michaels are more difficult but in a certain sense, we can write off one of the two, Ella's child. This Michael is the psychological offspring from Michael, Anna's lover in the other story. The child doesn't come to life very vividly. In any case, it is probably accurate to agree with less sympathetic critics that Lessing's children, not only in *The Golden Notebook* but in her later novels and short stories, are not her strongest figures, perhaps because children are not too subtle in concealing their true selves.

The adult Michael, the two Pauls and Saul have different physical characteristics, and different degrees of cowardice and nobility. Paul, the airman on duty at Mashopi, is something of a Greek figure, a hero with a tragic ending that is certainly ignoble but still "upper class." Ella's Paul has inherited the first Paul's self-distrust but hasn't been trained to control it. He is not "upper class." He is more romantic.

In the repetitions of the blue notebook we learn again with a variation that Michael is a doctor like the second Paul, but also a man whose father and mother perished in gas chambers. He is unquestionably "working class," compassionate, down to earth and "modern."

Saul is an extension of Paul and at the same time a **parody** of all the others, a man so modern that he sadly deceives himself. (Here, in reverse, is the biblical **allusion** to Paul who was first called Saul.)

Somewhat ironically (here the reason for the repetition begins to appear), all of these men are childlike, particularly Michael who is the "fiercest" male child. It seems as though Anna subconsciously connects him with still another child, her Janet. This "little girl, the eight-year old represents for him partly women - other women, whom he betrays to sleep with me; and partly child; the essence of child, against whom he is asserting his rights to live. He never speaks of his own children, without a small, half-affectionate, half-aggressive laugh - "his heirs, and his assassins." The **irony** rests in the fact that in portraying this adult small brother, Lessing has given us the "essence of child" but not indeed a child.

## TRUTH DESTROYED

Because Anna caught herself writing "fiction" in her notebooks, she decided to keep a factual diary. "Today he came into the kitchen...this started...he paid... I intervened..." After noting such humdrum events for a few days, Anna discovered that one doesn't recall all the facts and in the very act of selecting one or the other, nothing but the truth is certainly not the whole truth. There is a difference between "My mother was married to my father for a year, then divorced" and "My mother lived with my father for three years; then decided to have a baby and married so I should not be illegitimate, then divorced."

It was easier to write about Willi in the black notebook than to write about Max, her husband, in the true blue. What mattered in her case was that the marriage was canceled out and a "marvelous baby remained." All true, except perhaps the word "marvelous." This word reminds us of the "fictional" father and his baby and the not so "marvelous" fictional Ella. The twist in the story is that, to the child's father, and not to his fictional image, marriage was actually important. To the fictional father love and happiness came first.

An earlier note in the same diary had been more comprehensive. It talked about the event of the baby's conception. Because the couple on the other side of the wall had a baby whose crying didn't disturb their happy love-making, Max had said that having a baby might bring them together again. So they were married the next week. But marriage didn't bring the return of love. Later Max married someone else and Anna fell in love with Michael.

Once, after Michael taunted her that, when she scribbled in her notebooks, she didn't know what was true or false, Anna decided then and there to write down fully and completely the exact events of one single day. In the day she wrote about we recognize bits of happenings we have already encountered in other notebooks. Supposedly the truth will out but Anna, in a vein reminiscent of Virginia Woolf, indulges in considerable "inner monologizing." Her monologues tend to dramatize the non-Woolfian details of events such as the sights and smells that coincide with the arrival of her monthly period. Such scarcely pretty facts then throw our comparisons off and we recall the "new French" writers and Beckett's Molloy series. If in the amalgam of the two styles, Woolf's and Beckett's, Anna's truth becomes suspect, we can nevertheless recognize a highly perceptive semblance of true life.

Anna and Anna's day are very real. Both are complicated. In the subtleties of life the truth resides. All of the reader's brains and all of his five senses take in that day. It becomes an accolade to Doris Lessing's genius.

## CRIME

"There is some kind of social process involved which makes words like crime stupid." In this, an instant of insight, Anna (possibly Lessing herself) illuminated anew the whole subject of Good and Evil - the **theme** of nearly the entire body of Western Literature from the Hebraic Adam and Eve, King David, Judas; from the Hellenic Menelaus, Paris, Helen, Oedipus; from Milton's Devil, Goethe's *Faust*; to Golding's pig in *Lord of the Flies*.

"There is no right, no wrong, simply a process, a wheelturning." This sentence is brought on as a result of Anna's conceptualizing fresh, lively, young people as being dictated to by "hardened, fossilized" old men. The dryness, the deadness - the evil - "could not exist without the lively shoots of fresh life, to be turned so fast in their turn, into dead sapless wood."

But Anna cried out against such a view. It reminded her of one of her nightmares. In it a man was up against a wall about to be executed when there was a shift in the street-fighting and the roles changed. The executioner, not the victim, was against the wall. After shooting their former officer, the men of the firing squad went off to get drunk cursing and hating the man who had been bound but who was then free just as if he were the dead man. The wheel had turned.

No longer was the question one of good and evil. The crime was stupidity - the stupidity of the social process - the changing of roles. It seemed that good and evil were just words - merely useful to make swift judgments - to distinguish sweet dreams from nightmares - useful but stupid.

## COMMUNIST CLOUD-CUCKOO SPIT

Even though Anna will miss the association of her Communist friends ("people who had spent their lives in a certain kind of atmosphere, where it is taken for granted that...lives must be related to a central philosophy"), she has to admit there has been an intellectual collapse within the Party. Its internationalism had been killed by "the desperate, crazed spirit of struggle for survival to which we now give the name Stalinism."

Michael, the realist who still dreamt of the Nazis murdering his family, pointed out to Anna that her unpaid service to the Communist Party was in the British upper-class tradition in which her grandmother "worked for the starving poor." At the same time, he, the worker, could assign the success of her muckraking novel to "the capitalist publishing racket." It is ironic that Butte, Anna's boss in the office of the publishing outfit where she volunteered, came from an upper-middle-class background.

In the course of her job of reading, Anna objected to a particular manuscript which the Party chiefs had already decided to publish. It gave the impression that England was "locked in deep poverty, unemployment, brutality" and that English workers were all Communist or at least recognized the Communist Party as their spokesman.

This is the very same manuscript that Jack, the lower-echelon editor, described as Communist cloud-cuckoo spit. Naturally, one wonders about the P in spit, but not about Anna's disillusionment.

Anna herself was out of touch with working-class reality when she suddenly quit her job. How many workers grow dissatisfied but are unable to quit their jobs because they need the money? Anna could quit "suddenly" only because she had financial security which she somewhat haughtily claimed never worried her. She contended she could always get a job. This quality, or deficiency, in her personality will surface again when her relationship with Molly's affluent ex-husband is examined. The highly sensitive Anna could be blind.

## WHO AM I; WHO IS HE

When she tried to record the exact events of "her" day, Anna suspected that she was thinking more clearly. Nevertheless, she was still plagued with the question Who Am I which has nagged Everyman since Oedipus' anguished cry. Almost at once the next question Lessing proposes is on a high level - Who is he? Who is this other fellow who asks, "Who am I?"

Michael was the ex-Communist, the traitor who had quit, the lost soul. Jack was the Communist bureaucrat who, because he was a party member, had to share in the responsibility for the murder of Michael's old comrades. Mike the traitor was Anna's deceitful loved one and Jack the murderer was the good decent man whom she trusts. There is little wonder that Anna had nightmares about firing squads and captives who exchange roles.

Jehovah's glorification of the divine (Himself), "I am that I am", goes back to the book of Exodus. Even so, rational thinkers have always found the proposition difficult. Calling it the law of identity did not help their thinking until the law of contradiction was formalized. "A is not non-A." Because the number of Non-A's can easily be seen to be limitless, understanding the existence of the Non-A's can accordingly identify, limit, fix the A. A achieves his identity only through the Non-A's - the others - the He's. Who he is answers Who am I.

Otherness is a particular brand of Lessing's humanism. All her characters, singly and in amalgam, are specialized tools, well honed - particularly Anna. She achieves her identity through the others, as do they through her.

## BETRAYED BY HISTORY

It has often been said that the essence of tragedy is the catharsis it brings about. When a tragedy is witnessed, one is relieved at its end. "There but for the grace of God go I."

In this avowal, which Anna made and linked to the dream-story of the exchanged victims of the firing squad, she admitted the importance of the accidents of her position, the events of her own personal background.

What happens in all but one's immediate past seems always to have been accidental - the result of chance. A coin is flipped and we say "God only knows" why it came out heads or tails. It's just luck. We also speak of the wheels of chance - wheels indicating the transformation of chance into a process.

A realization of the process, the movement of all the phases and aspects of life is prerequisite to grasping Lessing's philosophy. She never preaches. She is never argumentative. She never says such and such is so and everything else false. Not being dogmatic, she can attest to the unknowable - which some people call "luck." In the pursuit of truth she seems to go even further agreeing with the poet Wallace Stevens that "God and the imagination are one."

Since the nineteenth century when Karl Gauss, the German mathematician, promoted the "normal" or "Bell-shaped" curve or theory of probability, the modern world has been able to speak of the laws of chance. It has been said that had the

Greeks known about this curve, a thing of beauty, they would have deified it. The Roman Fortuna, or Dame Fortune, would have been transcended. The probability curve is beautiful, too, because it is encouraging. It is a happy thing to realize that even if you are but a single coin being tossed one way or another, you are part of a law.

We can understand Anna's sympathy toward bad luck, in particular the bad luck of Jack, the Communist bureaucrat. He is described as "...intellectual. And decent. And yet behind him, part of him like myself, the miserable history of blood, murder, misery, betrayal lies." His was the misfortune of being born in the early thirties when almost all western thinkers were at least "a little bit pink." It wasn't his good luck, as it was Anna's, to be able to walk out of the Party and be able to say, "I'm shedding my skin, or being born again."

It is to Mrs. Lessing's credit that she sees the connection between humanism and the laws of science. Many scientists no longer think of cause and effect as links in a chain. They think about events in "fields" of different forces. Lessing does not analyze a human being in a series of pieces. She puts the pieces together so that a character has an organic meaning - a whole - not a collection but a Gestalt. We become aware that Mrs. Lessing is widely read in psychology. She is not an echo of old-fashioned behavioristic stimulus-and-response theory. She is not a scientific fundamentalist but an experimenting humanist.

## BLACK AND BLUE

Halfway through the blue notebooks where Anna had hoped to be strictly factual and honest, her mood gets (to paraphrase Swinburne) blacker than bluer. She had not yet realized that attempts at honesty can only relate to verifiable events whereas honesty, a concept, must remain illusive. In her blueness she failed to appreciate how her attempts had changed her. In not achieving what she had expected she ignored the value of the heuristic. Out of the fear of dishonesty, she drew a heavy black line across the continuing pages of her diary entries. The notes in her tidy small handwriting gave way to undated hurriedly written comments that were sometimes unintelligible.

It was as if Anna recognized the danger of recording her life in daily sequential parts. She thought she could avoid the danger by selecting self-sufficient parts, though discontinuous. Finally, the idea of the whole being greater than the sum of its parts reawakened in her. The parts gave significant meaning to the whole. The truth rested in the fact that the whole achieved reality only from the direct representation of the parts even if they were accidental or even because they were accidental.

Anna saw many of the events she recorded as accidents or coincidences. A coincidence, she decided, was the coming together of certain events and nothing more. She resented the "nothing more." It gave her the blues. She felt a necessity to put things together. It was out of this need that she went on scribbling. The law of necessity engendered understanding. In the last pages of the blue notebook the tone of voice changed.

Anna began to be cognizant of a sense of history. A sensibility that, as Lessing points out even more emphatically in her writing after *The Golden Notebook*, is absent in politicians but is essential to statesmen or any admirable person. History must be more than a collection of verifiable facts because it can never be all the facts. It has to be a creative drive towards the future, grown out of the past. If the facts are limited, as they were in a section of Anna's diary entries, the result could be used only as propaganda.

Who can read Anna's entries and news clippings as anything but propaganda? Some hostile critics of *The Golden Notebook* were quick to apply the propaganda label. In their hasty reading (a common disease among reviewers), they missed the point that Anna herself saw the falsity in her entries and indeed shifted her stance. The moment of truth occurred in the shift which is an unrecorded drama in itself. It changed her from propagandist to prophet.

## FISHING FOR MEMORIES AND LOOKING BACKWARD

Anna once complained to Mother Sugar that so much time in their sessions together was spent in making her conscious of certain physical facts that she spent her childhood learning to ignore "so as to live at all."

Anna forgot that one discovers ancient myths in one's dreams - an old folk-lore in a father-relationship - the meaning of old sayings and proverbs. These could be more potent than the "analysis" of dreams themselves. They need not be made "relevant." It seemed that Mother Sugar was most pleased with her patient when she recognized the primitive in her. Without such an awareness Anna could not become clinically healthier or morally better. Fortunately Anna could joke about her puzzlements. This the analyst interpreted as a good sign.

## ICARUS

Anna confessed to Mother Sugar that in certain dreams she had experienced a kind of joy never felt when she was awake. In one such dream the mythical Icarus came to life. In the ancient myth, Icarus escaped from Crete on the artificial wings his father Daedalus had made for him. In the exultation of his flying he forgot the warning and flew too close to the sun, which melted the wax that secured his wings. Icarus crashed into the Aegean sea.

In the various aspects of the story several universal "truths" emerge. For Anna the joy of her dream came from the fact that the horror in Icarus' fall was contained in the story. It was a story. Stories cannot hurt. She was safe. Because of this, her dream was joyful in its tragedy.

It was not by accident that Lessing incorporated this myth in her novel. Her profound longing for peace after violence, safety after destruction, and her yearning for a non-violent world demanded a pattern. Icarus whirling and twirling with his silly wings, held on by impotent wax, is a comic figure, then tragic in fall. Finally, he becomes a healing figure in the sense of "There but for the grace of God go I." The major incidents of Anna's life followed this pattern. She is consciously fashioned as was Icarus and at the same time she is the fashioner, Daedalus. Hers is a story within a story that illustrates the tension of rest and movement, of Being and Becoming. It is an instruction in which Anna is both story-teller and witness, teacher and pupil, in the most useful of the arts, the art of life.

In the use of Icarus, Doris Lessing has solved a problem that confronts every artist: how to make one's vision of life understood by one's audience. In seeking an instrument to bring her meaning within the powers of the reader, Mrs. Lessing was not merely inspired by the Icarus myth as a safe dream but was utilizing all the critical knowledge resulting from her tremendous reading and the continuous exercise of putting words on paper. The voluminousness of her earlier novel, the pages and pages she has written - inspired, critical, visionary or technical - turn readers into receiving vessels where they can contain some small truths, having spilled out pretense, selfishness, and stupidity.

## PUTTING THE PAIN AWAY

When Anna heard her lover say that if they had nothing else in common, they had sex, the pit of her stomach went cold. Real cramps produced by an emotional state?

On "that" diary day when it was obvious that Anna was not pregnant, the omission of any mention of contraception, vasectomy, or any other temporary or permanent sterilization procedure raises once more the unsolved psychological query, "Does Anna suffer pain because she is afraid of pregnancy or because she wishes she were pregnant?"

Since she was a woman who enjoyed good health, the only kind of doctor she saw was the psychiatrist, Mother Sugar. What had pained her most was the fact that she couldn't feel - emotionally. Mother Sugar prescribed putting the pain away by putting it into the past - where it couldn't hurt. Forget your troubles, recognize one part after another of your life, recent or early, as an aspect of general human experience. To this Anna objected. She believed that she was living the kind of life no woman had ever lived before. Her experiences were new.

Admitting that there had been artist-women before, independent women and women who had insisted on sexual freedom, Anna asserted, nevertheless, that she was not like such women because they didn't "wake up terrified by a dream of the H-Bomb exploding...hatred and fear and envy and competition every minute of the night and day..."

Anna insisted that even though total destruction was blatantly possible, the golden age should then, for the same reason and for the first time, be possible. "I want to be able to separate in myself what is old and cyclic, the recurring history, the myth from what is now, what I feel or think that might be new."

Anna was making progress with Mother Sugar who was confident she would soon be writing more than notebook scribblings. She had reached beyond the Platonic idea that the body is a prison of the soul but still didn't quite know how to define "soul." She had not caught up with Aristotle who said the body is an instrument of life, a potential for the soul. She loved Michael and didn't worry too much about the body or the soul. He told her that if the sex is not sick, one is unaware of the body. One is conscious only of the body when something is wrong. All this she had learned but she still searched to understand what makes the body forget or makes one forget the body.

Scientists investigate the body and its processes but the artist must discover what transcends the body - what both Plato and Aristotle called the soul. Anna had not reached that point of comprehension.

The paradox of I and Thou, the praying man and his God, became for Anna the paradox of the artist and his audience. The common sense of life had taught her there were thousands of "thous" in her audience. Her mind was tumbling with stories of those thousands but she couldn't cross the bridge to them. Art, her creative spirit, may have lost its power but Anna kept herself open.

## FORM AND DISCONTENT

If what you have to say matters, then it must, as has been said many times, take form. Formlessness implies that nothing counts. To say that Beckett is formless is to label him as a nihilist.

In one of the most cogent discussions between Anna and Mother Sugar, Lessing's literary creed is laid face up on the table. The chances are that formless writing will not be art. Its appeal will be limited. Conscious form is an inherent part of *The Golden Notebook's* very subtle structure. The importance of the story is thereby paid a compliment. The message is strengthened by its form. It has value for many kinds of readers, not only the aristocratic few. Doris Lessing is not what English and American literati used to call a "Brahmin."

Whereas rhetoric has as its purpose to stir an audience to action, the purpose of art is to bring out the viewer's, the listener's, the reader's gift of understanding and sympathy. Art focuses on the tranquil moment when the reader responds. No one would ever say of Lessing's work, "That's so much rhetoric." She is too much concerned with the art of life - happiness. What has discontent to do with happiness? We can find the answer if we first make a distinction between matrix form and developmental form. In matrix form a work is divided usually in classical sections - say twenty-four; there are a beginning, sometimes in the middle, and an end; usually the muses and the audience are invoked; a purpose is stated. In developmental form there is usually a journey. Matrix form is centripetal. Developmental form is centrifugal.

*The Golden Notebook* is an example of developmental form. A woman whose life is a mess and whose work is meaningless to her passes from one mental way-station to another. Though she is supposed to be a free woman her past and her now "bind," with many reversals. Her story is punctuated by flashes of insight and telling symbols. Through this form the discontent recounted in the notebooks climaxes in a golden break-through - the golden novel within the novel. Discontent has paid off.

## CATERPILLARS

In the black notebook, having to do with Africa, attention was called to anteaters, butterflies, grasshoppers, and other insects. And later on we had the ironic, if sadly humorous account of the London pigeon. In the blue notebook, the true fact diary, such symbolic accounts could seem out of place. However, when Anna was at the lowest ebb of her writing, not merely because the truth is illusive but also because words have failed her, she jotted down one of her most illuminating similes. Straight forward prose writing, the writing used in instruction books, police court records, the writing resulting from mechanical inputs, proved inadequate to her purpose. A machine cannot suffer from a "vertigo of words."

Anna was scarcely a machine. She was a being who was trying to describe "a state of being." When her "being" had no place to go but up, when being must be becoming, she was forced into a figure of speech, the simplest of them all, the **simile**. In this case she went so far as to introduce one **simile** with another.

"Anna, as a pulse in a great darkness..." "As a pulse" is vague but the feeling of throbbing is there. What beats? How does a caterpillar move - forward? - by pulsating?

This **simile** progresses. "As a pulse in a great darkness, and the words that I, Anna, write down are nothing, or like the secretions of a caterpillar that are forced out in ribbons to harden in the air."

She doesn't say her words are like caterpillars that will become butterflies but we notice she says her words are like the "secretions" of a caterpillar. But somehow Anna must have felt the inadequacy of this simile. This particular figure of speech did not complete her thought. The tension of art, the tension under which any artist writes, drove her, not just her pen, from **simile** into **metaphor**. She did not write "the secretions are forced out like ribbons" which would have contained a third **simile** but "the secretions are forced out in ribbons."

In assimilating these short sentences, a reader can learn not merely the difference between **simile** and **metaphor**, but he may grasp a lesson in aesthetics, perhaps even a lesson on a deeper level in psychology. Anna in the blue notebook appears in the blackest of moods. She could not go lower. What could be closer to the earth than the caterpillar? The story of Adam and Eve, sin and the crawling snake has surfaced again in the soul of a new poet.

## NAMING

"Give a name to it," said Mother Sugar to Anna when she had a particular dream sequence. It had been a nightmare about a vase that had a personality that was anarchistic and destructive. The figure dancing and jumping like a pixie menaced everything that was alive. Anna "named" the dream, Destruction.

The importance of naming cannot be undervalued. Books have been written on this fascinating subject. Attendant rituals have been formalized when names are given to persons. No religion is lacking in naming ceremonies. Naming, inherent in all speech forms, distinguishes man from all other animals - a distinction that flatters, that cajoles, that growls, that scraps and fights. Naming also exorcizes. Anna's nightmare was "purified" as soon as it was named. She dreamt it again and again with slight variations. Each time she gave it a name, always in negative terms, nothing good. "Perhaps," Mother Sugar continued, "as you dream deeper, you'll feel the vitality as good as well as bad."

Anna did, indeed, dream deeper. Instead of dreaming of an inhuman figure which she recognized as evil qualities causing her to wake up screaming, the figure became a person whom she did not recognize at first; "then I understood that this terrible malicious force was in that person who was a friend." Being able to "name" the person terrified her the more because she saw that what was loose in the "other" person was loose in herself. At first she was being sucked into further danger but then she felt (as Mother Sugar predicted) she could deal with it and be safe. "The thinking Anna can look at what Anna feels and name it."

Anna had demonstrated to herself that the power to name is the power to transcend. Once named the quality the name symbolizes disappears. The process is not a little awesome. It is difficult for mankind to admit this. The God of the Bible actually forbade the fixation on images and names. God would disappear if we could name Him. God remains anonymous (unnamed) in an abundance of many names - God, the father, God, the bridegroom, God, the judge, God the thunderer, God (or Goddess) of Wisdom, and so forth. Even Isis so "named" by the Egyptians is called "father," "brother," "mother." Certain Australians call Him not just "father" but "grandfather," "uncle," "elder brother." The additive quality of the symbol can be recognized in idols with ten heads or ten breasts.

It seems that God doesn't want to be identified. A man does. If man can "name," he first identifies, then loses the identity, and then leaps into another cycle. It is this process that Mother Sugar recognized and tried to teach Anna. Anna got a glimmer of it. She began to see an "unfolding" in her life. The creative was awakening, still perhaps in her dream world, but awakening.

On a practical level, Anna took a big step forward as a result of her naming experience. For five years she had been a woman she could now name. She had been a woman "terribly vulnerable, critical, using femaleness as a sort of standard or yardstick to measure and discard men.... I...invited defeat from men without even being conscious of it. (But I am conscious of it. And being conscious of it means I shall leave it all behind me and become - but what?) I was stuck fast in an emotion common to women of our time, that can turn them bitter, or Lesbian, or solitary. Yes, that Anna, during that time was..." Here she draws a heavy black line over what she had written.

## THE WALLS ARE THIN

When Anna was tired or particularly distressed, she said that the walls of herself were thin. What she means by this is not clear. It is as ambiguous as John Donne's "No man is an island." In one sense no man is an island because he is involved with all other human beings. In another sense every man is an island, ever alone with himself because no man can achieve total communication with another.

In Anna's case we may ask if she was saying her walls were thin because they protected her but thinly from the dangers of the world. Rather was she indeed in a state where her sense and sensibility were going to break through her thin walls. She was to be isolated within herself no longer - Isole - island!

Once more she was going to begin to write, write about what she felt deeply. Creative force within her was bursting and it hurt. As Mother Sugar has sensed it, the reader senses the breaking of the thin wall. Anna's dried up walls were beginning to send messages.

The **metaphor** of the thin wall seems to be subconsciously ready for extension. An imaginative reader can leap into the extension. He can guess it, and be intrigued by a possible new story that is developing. Metaphorically in Anna's case, the hymen is to be ruptured again.

## JEWS AND RUSSIANS

Anna's search for the truth is highlighted by the appearance of the character she has named Nelson. Ironically, Lessing has given this name, made famous by the hero of Trafalgar, to a Jewish-American. Anna first met him at a Communist meeting of intellectuals gathered in Molly's living room. What they heard about the state of Communism from the speakers was bad but nothing that could not have been read in the newspapers. Ten persons remained after the formal meeting. Anna should have left with the others because by that time she had already left the Party. The small group asked questions and the answers descended (or ascended) to a new level of truth - truth about horror, torture, beatings. The murder of Jews in frightful ways was spoken of from firsthand witnesses in the tones of quiet restrained Britishers. Then Nelson arose and spoke with passion. His oratory had obviously grown out of professional political experience. Vehemently he told them the Communist Parties of the west would collapse because they were incapable of telling the truth. The conditions of the Soviet Communist

Party should be brought to light honestly. The lesser truths that had been fed the open meeting of forty-odd were acceptable for presentation to those who could only take the less horrible. The leaders were so long used to this technique that they could not themselves know true from false. As a consequence their downfall was inevitable. In accusing the "insiders" of lies and yet condoning the use of "mild" truth, Nelson put himself in an untenable position. He launched into more violent accusations. He became hysterical.

The atmosphere reminded Anna of the onset of her dream "destruction." She got up to leave. She passed Molly in the kitchen where Molly was crying. Molly said, "It's all very well for you, you aren't Jewish."

When Anna reached the street she found Nelson had followed her. He was quiet again and offered to take her home. Because we know she was attracted to him, we immediately sense, although Lessing is too much of an artist to tell us, that Anna's dream which Mother Sugar had foretold might augur for her a good within the evil. After recording her first meeting with Nelson, Anna drew still another heavy black line blocking out what she wrote, probably very truthfully, in her blue notebook. The reader is perhaps learning in a very subtle way that the truth is a private thing.

## AVERTING THE EVIL EYE

Midway in the ugly scene describing the American "show-biz" people, Lessing uses another enlightening **simile**. "It was like peasants touching amulets to avert the evil eye."

The first of the keywords is "peasants." Lessing's Americans in this scene are peasants. They are "nice people with an instinct for generosity." They were loud and noisy. Their self-assurance was superficial. "They have a nervous frightened look to their shoulders." Their humor was self-punishing. They got loaded to help face the social event ahead of them. (How many Americans take a drink before they go to a party?) They covered up for each other. They tried to get as much drink inside of them as quickly as possible. What is this evil eye these peasants felt they had to free themselves from? Their own limitations? It is here that we feel the substance of what Lessing's view of one-hundred-percenters is. She tells us that Americans don't set limits on themselves. They seem to want space, physical and mental, that is without boundaries. This is an admissible characteristic. But trouble sometimes comes when their want is too great. It can make them anxious, frantic. They seem so aware of the possibility of failure. It makes them self-conscious. They are apt to feel that humor and high spirits will save them. Humor is their "amulet." Unfortunately this humor is frequently self-denigrating. It can make them disgusted with themselves. It is as if peasant-like they beat themselves with sudden laughter - a laughter to disinfect themselves - to take the pain away - to exorcize it.

When Anna thought about these Americans, and Anna pondered over all her associations, she reached a certain truth, to be sure about one American among many. She concluded that this man and his wedded wife, regardless of herself or any other mistress, were "bitterly close," Americans were tied to each other in neurotic pain-giving - "pain dealt and received; pain as an aspect of love, apprehended as a knowledge of what the world is, what growth is." This idea is reminiscent of the flowering branch, the talisman Mother Sugar told Anna to use when she was "on her own."

## MADNESS

"He (Nelson) went off, shouting and screaming at me - at women. An hour later he telephoned me to say he was sorry, he was nuts and that was all there was to it." It becomes obvious that one of the reasons this particular American was "neurotic" was the possibility of failing at loving. "Believe me, I wanted nothing more than to have the real thing with you.... If the love they say is possible is more real than what we seem to get...."

Anna was terribly hurt. She felt the atmosphere of the dream - the ambience of destruction. She dreamt the dream again with still another variation. It was as if she were having a telephone conversation with Nelson although he was in the same room. He was warm, yet grudging. As she talked to him, she "could feel the beginning of the smile, the smile of joyful spite. I even made a few dancing steps, the head jerking, almost doll-like stiff dance of the animated vase...so now I am the evil vase; next I'll be the old man-dwarf; then the hunch-backed old woman - then what?" She could hear Nelson scream down the telephone, "the witch."

This dream she named "joy in destruction" and didn't dream it again. It had been a "neurotic" dream about her "neurotic" American but, awake and alive in the days following the dream, she experienced a change. Anna came close to genuine madness. (In Lessing's later novel, *The Four-Gated* City, we have not only a mad woman who is confined but also a main character who at one point induces herself into madness.)

Anna had been so wounded by Nelson that the fear of being rejected again by a man, the fear of sexual failure on her part, became so intense that she felt like running. She, however, recognized her own cowardice. As if she needed an amulet to exorcize her fear (she had evidently forgotten Mother Sugar's flowering talisman), she allowed herself to drift into an affair with the disgusting, prostitute-teasing man from Ceylon - the perverted, sadistic DeSilva.

Anna is quite mad when she recognizes in his sly smile the smile from the figure in her dreams. "I wanted to run out of the room. And yet I was thinking. This quality, this intellectual 'I wanted to see what was going to happen, I want to see what will happen next' is something loose in the air, it is in so many people one meets, it is in me. It is part of what we all are. It is the other face of: It doesn't matter, it didn't matter to me."

The love-making that could matter to Anna had been pushed far in the past. "It belonged to the Anna who was normal." To reach a point where one can say love-making doesn't matter is madness. When Anna comprehended this, she felt drained and lifeless but her sanity was in control. When she gave DeSilva breakfast, the reader seems to get the feeling that Anna also knows that even what one eats matters. One remembers Ella, in the yellow notebook, saying to herself after Paul has left her, "Being mad is not being able to stop yourself doing something that you know is irrational."

# THE GOLDEN NOTEBOOK

## FREE WOMEN

..................................................................

It is an eye-opener to come upon quotations from a book very popular, since its publication in 1966, with students and educational psychologists which are formalizations of concepts contained in Doris Lessing's *The Golden Notebook*: Harvard's Jerome S. Bruner developed in his book *Toward a Theory of Instruction* a six-point rubric on how people keep on learning. He has much to say about "strategies," "patterns of experience," and the form and logic of "conceptualization." The last of his pronouncements says what our novelist knew and put to use years before, that as a person grows he has an increasing capacity to deal with more than one subject at a time and that he can handle several sequences covered in the same period of time. In her structuring of *The Golden Notebook*, Lessing did not hesitate to put multiple demands on readers who she was convinced would never stop growing. The form her novel takes is a very subtle compliment a reader can but appreciate.

Each section in each notebook which is preceded by a section concerning the life of the notebook writer is not a mere skipping around for the sake of suspense build-up, even though this is one result. When Lessing takes us again and again away from the notebook and into Anna's life, we get a keener sense of vitality. It is as though the stories in the notebooks needed correction.

The searching and questing process within the notebooks had to be related to the accidents of life which are beyond personal control.

Even though the notebooks are written in terms of what people do and think, the language in "The Free Women" pieces is subtly different. The speed of life, its intense drama, seem to demand the very "shorthand" language that Lessing contrived.

## TENSION

There is an obvious difference between reporting events in a notebook after they have happened and hearing Molly scream that Tommy shot himself. The difference is between reading, let's say listening, and hearing. We forget all about the art of writing, we forget about chaos and order, we forget about behaviorism and cognitive psychology, we forget about dreams and imagination, we forget about truth and lies. We hear the scream. We see the blood trickling down the stairs. We don't say, "I'll think about it," but "I'll be right over."

Among The Blind, The One-Eyed Is King. In Sophocles' *Oedipus the King*, blind Teiresias is the prophet who could see into the future. He is not the King. Oedipus, who was so wrong about the past, the present and the future, was King. When Oedipus is blind, he is no longer King. The one-eyed of the world can be Kings. They can fight to the death with other half-see-ers - but over the blind they win.

When Tommy went blind, he developed a sixth sense. He learned to make his own coffee without burning himself and without spilling it. He could sense Anna's presence in a room. He could "see" an eyebrow lift with a change of voice. He could "sense" her desire to leave and raise himself up but he couldn't stop her.

For a time his power over people was increased. His hearing seemed more acute. Because Tommy was always at home, Molly had to call Anna from an outside 'phone. He moved down from an upstairs bedroom to the large living-room where Molly could no longer entertain, certainly not a male visitor. She had to shop for him, get regular meals. She had to give up meetings and seeing her friends. His friends, including those who came to read to him, were the only ones she saw in her own home.

He was also more powerful because he had time to think. He could put his finger on so many weaknesses - point out so many of the blind spots in the world - the public world and also the private world. He became the person he had always wanted to be. He became a happy person with all the power of a happy person. It shocked Molly that his enjoyment of his situation could be irritating to her. How could she be miserable when for the first time in his life he was all of one piece with himself? The mockery of "one piece" when his mutilated eyes stared at her made her weep in her entire body. It was the mother, not the blind son, who came to the conclusion that "life is getting used to things that are really intolerable."

## TOMMY AND REGGIE GATES

On the night before he tried to kill himself, and in his clumsy way succeeded only in blinding himself, Tommy went over to

Anna's and asked, "What are we alive for?" When she couldn't answer his question, which was also an appeal, his triumphant laughter scared her. In a fumbling way she tried to suggest that his powerful father could get him any number of jobs, anywhere in the world; his mother could launch him in social work; Anna, in the literary field.

Anna was the wrong person to give advice. She, the free woman, who had the freedom to make so many choices, had been forced by their very number into stoicism and Tommy was no stoic.

"A hundred things to do," he said, "but only one thing to be." Then he continued obstinately, "But perhaps I don't feel myself worthy of such a wealth of opportunity... Anna - have you met Reggie Gates?"

Reggie Gates was the milkman's son, a scholarship student. If he passed his exams, he would be upper-middle-class like Tommy. If he failed, he would deliver milk for the rest of his life. He had no choice. It would be one thing or the other. That was the system and he thought that those who complained about it were "barmy." So he was a Tory and wasn't suffering a "paralysis of will."

This was the sickness Tommy feared he had. It was so like Tommy to take the phrase personally. Anna suspected that the phrase had been used by the boy's father - primarily in a public sense. The father, with his ex-wife and Anna in mind, had accused Communist Party members, both ex- and still active, of being megalomaniacs. He had pointed out to his son that the reds, given the opportunity to set up a clinic for some unfortunates in some outlying part of the world, would refuse, saying, "What's the point of improving the health of fifty people when the basic organization is unchanged?"

Such a reply would have indeed been a symptom of "paralysis of the will." What the boy's father had actually said was that people can't be bothered. Unless they could see a complete change in two or three years as had happened in Russia and China, people became lethargic. There was no point in running around being political. They will had become paralyzed.

Needless to say, Anna, on this night when he was to put an end to his own paralysis of will, tried to defend humanity. With a great intellectual effort, the only kind of effort she knew, Anna's "stoicism" appeared to transcend philosophy. "It seems to me something like this - every so often, perhaps once in a century. There's a sort of act of faith." She continued to indicate that in some country or other at various intervals there occurs a big thrust forward. It is a faith in what is possible, an act of imagination strong enough to be translated into deeds. An end to being animals. There would always be those without paralysis of will. "One must have faith. Trumpets and fanfares."

While Anna talked, she also knew that Tommy had stolen looks into her notebook, and knew, through them, that she, Anna, too had suffered what he was suffering. She had dried up in her writing, taken to cutting out newspaper-clippings and pasting them in her notebooks. All she had seemed able to do was balance one chaotic event against another. She could only stare at a statement about thermal radiation, about megatons. How could she help this young man who had read that she herself had been completely beset by alternative viewpoints? He accused her of arrogance and irresponsibility. Was she cracking up?

## BE HAPPY IF IT KILLS YOU

Does this expression give you the "giggles"? Does its ultimate hedonism strike you as obscene? At several different points in the description of the visit Tommy paid Anna on that night, Lessing speaks of Tommy as giggling. It must occur to the reader that Tommy giggled because he was mad and that he attempted suicide because he was mad. On the other hand, it seems possible that Tommy giggled because he was laughing at people who tried so hard to be happy, people who deceived themselves, people who were so dishonest, even those whom he loved, that he didn't want to live with them any longer. Thinking he had seen the truth made him feel intensely happy with himself. He was so happy that it killed him (almost).

In this sense Tommy might giggle but he was also trying to be sympathetic to Anna. In telling her what's wrong with her, after he had read her secrets, he seemed genuinely desirous of comforting her. Giggling and helping don't go together. He was of two minds. A split mind is the simplest etymological definition of schizophrenia.

Tommy himself said that he was a failure because he never could make up his mind. He had too many choices. An admission of failure and a realization of its causes are not the conclusions of a madman unless failure drives one to madness. Because Tommy even fails at killing himself, the reader can't be sure Lessing was saying that Tommy was mad.

From the dialogue of that eerie night the question of Anna's sanity also arises. We have seen that she and Tommy are very much alike. She is a mixture of Molly and Richard in the sense that Tommy is the son of both. They are both examples of the type of solitary unattached persons who have become the non-heroes of much contemporary fiction. In having two loners in one story, Lessing explodes the over-simple treatment of the typical loner. Anna and Tommy are different in many ways, particularly in their degrees of madness and degrees of failure.

Failure is part of the atmosphere of madness. Anna is a failure at love and marriage. She is a failure, from her viewpoint, as a mother. Her child's desire to "conform" disappointed her. She feels a failure at her writing.

In several instances we have had references to the spiral figure. The going around and around seems like Tommy. The upward twist seems like Anna. The sucking figure, the gurgle of water down a trap, seems like Tommy. When the trap gets plugged, we have Anna. And finally the rippling figure - the stone that is thrown into the water and causes ever widening ripples. This figure applies to both.

Lessing, who could hardly be expected not to suffer from disillusionment after World War II, had been writing about failure in *The Landlocked*, the most recent volume in her series *The Children of* Violence. It is a study in the failing quest of the heroine of the series, Martha Quest. It is not inconceivable that Mrs. Lessing interrupted the series because her concept of failure had undergone a revision. *The Golden Notebook*, with its **theme** of failure which launches a quest for truth, stands by itself. It was only after *The Golden Notebook* that Lessing concluded the series with *The Four-Gated* City. In this last novel Martha Quest dies. The failure is the failure of a bombed-out science-fiction world, out of which evolves a new world.

That madness incipient in both Anna and Tommy is evident from what these two do not say to each other on the night of Tommy's shooting himself. It is their actions, their subconscious feelings, their very bodily movements that betray them.

When Tommy left her, she was in a "trough of exhaustion" but his madness had not totally submerged her. She had escaped. We have the feeling that the artist in her had saved her. The lack of it, the lack of creative power had sealed Tommy's doom. It is true Tommy continued to exist, but in his continued existence after the shot that failed he was forever blind. Anna, on the other hand, was richer for the experience at the edge of madness. In her continued existence she felt that the world would continue to exist.

Sometimes it's good to shout and scream. "Why not be depressed if you feel like it?" Anna's depression was a message from another part of her that said, "Keep on living." The creative artist of the notebooks was not dried up.

## MARION AND TOMMY

After the explosive scene with Anna, and Tommy had left, Marion staggered in. What then transpired gives us further insight into why Tommy is his mixed-up self. In the manner of so many drunks, Marion looked around Anna's room, and collapsed all her tired heavy flesh into a chair while Anna, slim, neat and tidy in black slacks and black shirt, sat opposite, but not for long. Marion was too tight to articulate but not tight enough to conceal her jealousy of Anna's freedom and way of life. In hissing spurts she compared herself, with all the sarcasm of a rich woman and a mother of wellborn sons, to the woman who could have affairs with one handsome man after another, perhaps including her own husband. Anna, who knew all Marion's vital statistics and all about her current problems, each checked out from different sources, all confidential, namely husband Richard, former wife Molly, and stepson Tommy, was too tired to listen. She wanted only to get Marion to bed but, since there was enough whisky in Marion to make her ugly and persistent, this took time. While Marion stumbled from one nasty comment to another, Anna thanked her lucky stars she didn't have to live with the false pretenses of Marion and Richard. Finally, Marion's chin began to drop on her chest. Only then was Anna able to roll her on to a bed. "Marion lay loose, her mouth open, her face wet with spittle and tears." This is the woman who afterward went with her husband to Tommy's bedside at the hospital. This is the woman whom the blind young man turned to instead of to his father and his own mother. This is the woman who bought him books, read to him, and spent hours with him, while Molly downstairs wondered with increasing irritation what was going on.

Tommy's interest in intellectual things, in politics and economic affairs, always too extensive as his father would say for his own good, increased with his blindness and the leisure time it enforced. Marion read and read and was more and more intrigued by Tommy's knowledge and talk. To some extent she reformed. Tommy had told her it was more courageous to drink a little than to drink not at all.

When next she came to see Anna, Marion presented a different image. She was well dressed, her eyes were lively, she appeared in control of herself. She bragged that, thanks to Tommy, she was taking a broader interest in life, particularly in politics. She looked roguish in a girlish way when she commented that her new interest was irritating not only to her mother and sisters, but also to her busy husband. His annoyance, in the light of the fact that his private life seemed to indicate that men of his class didn't take wives too seriously, struck her as bullying. She began to consider divorce, and to dress better. In confessing to Anna, she was not playing a role. She had reverted from dipsomaniac to stupid little girl. Her pursuit of knowledge with Tommy seemed more impetuous than earnest. Anna thought she preferred Marion as a lush, bitter, disillusioned, and truthful than the sober coy little school girl she had now to confront. Marion could talk about "good causes," "negative attitudes," and Africa as a "continent in chains." She could repeat the Communist **cliches** but Anna was more partial to a Marion who gave old clothes to the neighborhood poor.

Who was responsible for the change? Just Tommy? If Tommy had not gone blind, would he have turned toward Marion, would Marion have turned toward him? Was Tommy, in encouraging Marion to take up causes, to march in protests, to get arrested with demonstrators, merely laughing at his own liberal-minded communistic Jewish mother and her intellectual free woman friend, Anna? Was he merely punishing his father for his ability to concentrate on money-making? Was he jealous of his father's secretaries?

Anna searched for the answers. She knew Tommy was not mad. Nevertheless he seemed, in his preoccupation with Marion and her new interests, a sort of zombie. The physical damage of his blindness was inconsequential in comparison with his personality change. Meanwhile Anna had problems of her own. Her child was growing to adolescence. Her homosexual boarder was so obnoxious she had to insist, in spite of her ethical and moral qualms, upon his leaving. He couldn't get around her with flowers.... Anna's life kept right on going.

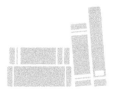

# THE GOLDEN NOTEBOOK

## THE GOLDEN NOTEBOOK

....................................................................

It is not easy to say what the *Golden Notebook* is all about. Interpretation will differ if one is under thirty trying to imagine what life will be like after fifty or if one is over fifty trying to remember life under thirty. It is true that this notebook purports to be a symbolic synthesis of the earlier ones. There are cinematographic flashbacks to the people and events at the Mashopi Hotel, a new review of Paul Tanner and Michael as two characters in one. Once more Anna's lover is the American, Saul Green, who came to rent a room in her flat at the end of the blue notebook. Once more there is sharp criticism of the American life style which once again is pardonable because of its penetrating honesty and somewhat humorous generosity. Much that is the same is subtly new. There certainly is at least one **theme** that, if not entirely new, comes to light in full force.

The style is compressed; the story more racy; the dreams more revealing; the philosophy sharper. The **parody** and **irony** are contained in not one but two short sketches. The last of these is in brackets and claims not to be written by Anna but by the young American. The notebook's very last line, still bracketed, reads: "(This short novel was later published and did rather well)."

## MIRROR, MIRROR ON THE WALL

In the opening pages Anna has just asked Saul why people, such as they, seem to want to experience everything, why they are driven to be as many different people as possible. Had there been such people in earlier times?

Saul told her that he didn't know the answers and didn't care about such. He wished only for deliverance from his drives. So, he went out. Then Anna's "illuminations" began. The room became a cage, with a tiger sitting on its top. Sometimes the tiger was a sleek beautiful animal resting quietly. Then it was vicious, slashing its tail about. The tiger became Saul. When men threatened the tiger, she didn't want him to be hurt. An admonisher in her dream told her to control her sleep, to stop playing with the tiger, to stop making up stories, to take another look at her past, to name the events to assure herself that her past was her own, was still there. She saw the Mashopi Hotel "in the wine-smelling moonlight," smelled eucalyptus trees, saw Maryrose and George Hounslow. She saw millions of white butterflies, in a big white flower unfolding like the explosion of a hydrogen bomb. She looked down to see at her feet grasshoppers inches deep.

Then Paul and Michael converged to become a new stronger figure. He told her that she was not a failure, she was a boulder pusher, a useful one. Then it was as if a new projectionist took over. She saw flicks of Paul and Ella, Michael and Anna, Julia, Molly, Tommy, Richard, even Doctor West. With the speed of the film they became distorted. She seemed to be the projectionist who had filmed them with all the wrong emphasis. Then a new projectionist seemed to take over. He showed her the Boothby daughter, June, who was "impelled by an outer power" to go to her man. In her sleep she must have heard Saul come back. She woke up and knew that it was he who had been the projectionist.

Just as Anna had become conscious of a new awareness, so the reader's mind is alerted to the new **theme**. It is the theme, or rather the generalization, that all men are driven - are "impelled by an outer power."

Saul and Anna are "driven" persons. Saul knows he is being driven, resents it but has accepted the fact. To live is to be driven. Anna had been driven without knowing it. Only little by little has she become conscious of the force that drives her to sex and that drives her to being a boulder-pusher. Like Saul, she makes no attempt to identify the force. Like Saul she resents it. Like Saul she knows she will always be driven as he is driven. Yet there is a subtle difference - perhaps the difference between the yin and the yang. Lessing elucidates the **theme** by turning from the general to the particular.

## THERE'S MY WIFE AND KIDS

This is an expression Saul claims his American countrymen use when they give up being pushers, when they give up being seekers, when they get to be over thirty. The wife and kids are an excuse. They stop driving. Put another way, the force that had driven them stops. Their idealism is gone. Their desire to make something of themselves is swept under the rug. Their hopes for a better world are buried in newsprint. Because youth seems to be worn out, its continuous existence is denied. The curse lies in the denial. Saul is somewhat bitter that he has not been able to fall into the pattern of his friends back home. He is indignant that they don't realize they have been cursed. What you don't know doesn't hurt you. It is sad Saul knows. It is too late for him not to know. The only time Saul says he has been really happy was when he was one of a gang of kids on the street corner. They believed they could change the world. Anna calls this hankering, American sentimentality. But Saul objects. The emotions the gang had were honest at the time. What was sad was that such emotions could be put away, buttoned up, disposed of.

When Saul asks, "What's going to happen to me, Anna?" she begins to smoulder. His egoism that stressed me in "happen to me" inflamed her. Why had he not asked, "What's going to happen to you?" or at least "What's going to happen to us?" His egoism was rubbing against hers.

## AN EXPLOSIVE SCENE

Anna insulted Saul by saying that he was going to leave off his cannibalism. He would feed no longer on one person after another. He would become a kind old man whom the young idealists of the future would turn to for advice. Every gentle old soul left behind him a trail of emotional crime. His past would be totally concealed in the bulging solidity of a middle-aged figure. Under his crew-cut and behind his spectacles, the small voice of "remember me" would become weaker and less frequent. He will forget his victims. Saul fought back. He had always been good for people. He shook them out of themselves. They hadn't been victims! They were what they were and he was what he was.

"I am what I am." Saul grew vehement in his own defence, his raving grew noisier. It was one continuous stream of I-I-I. Finally he looked at Anna, so much older than he, with all the priggishness of youth. He shouted, "Anna you're drunk" He was scandalized but just as quickly lustful. He took her quickly, rage descended, guilt ascended. He covered her up gently before he tip-toed away.

## THINKING IT OVER

Though Anna and Saul thought it over and concluded to the contrary, these two were good for each other. Each made the other aware of characteristics they have not assigned to themselves but saw in the other. They were forced to admit the traits they shared in common. What each admired in the other they could also see in themselves. It gave them much needed confidence in themselves. They had taken stands for and against the same ideas. Without putting it in words, they told each other how good they were not just for themselves but their world. At the same time each knew that their relationship had to be buttoned up, chalked up to experience, and put in the past.

It was Anna, the older, the more experienced, the more traveled, more widely read, who was first to realize that their roads would part. Perhaps it was the yin of it - the woman's intuition. Though she drove herself like a man and was driven as both man and woman can be driven, she never gave up as to the importance of chance. "The God only knows" viewpoint - the power of Lady Luck - Dame Fortune. The fact that these last two figures were female never seemed to have swung into Saul's orbit.

He has missed the point earlier when she had indicated that when a woman has a baby, when she feels it most that she is fulfilling her destiny, her very destiny is in the hands of chance. Will she have a boy or a girl? Anna had sensed and voiced her opinion that, if she had a boy-child in the room upstairs instead of Janet, Saul would not have felt invaded. He could have accepted another male in "their" household. Another woman should be an invasion against him. Anna knew that Janet was an inevitable infringement upon their union. The two adults were alike in that they could accept each other so long as there was no encroachment.

Saul never understood that part of Anna that belonged to Janet. No lover of hers ever had - even those with girl-children of their own. No one of these men had been more than slightly friendly to Janet. Only the homosexual boarder had read to her, and had shared in her imaginative life. He had so understood her that she had come to love him. In this Anna had seen a danger, perhaps too late for the child had begun to mix up the yin and the yang. Tommy had also been kind to her in his brotherly way but Tommy had himself been confused, perhaps more so because he still had a (divorced) father whereas Janet had none at all.

Saul had no need of Janet. She was a drag on him. But Janet was an anchorage for Anna. She was more than a mooring. She was a stabilizer. She was Anna's insurance against madness. She was a responsibility. Feeding, clothing, shielding Janet kept Anna sane. Anna, the free woman, might be free from economics and free from the raised eyebrows of society but she was never free from chance - the chance that Janet was born a female, which brought responsibility for another human being. Freedom without responsibility meant madness. Motherhood was her emotional haven.

At the same time Anna recognized that responsibilities should not consume a person. She could sympathize with Saul's animosity to the phrase, "There's the wife and kids." She could understand both his drive and what was driving him. Still she knew she had to let him go. She could name what she had experienced with him. She could be safe.

Saul? He didn't want safety. To him the phrase, "There's the wife and kids," was an unmanly emotional retreat. A new horizon always had to beckon.

# THE GOLDEN NOTEBOOK

## LITERARY PARALLELS AND NON-PARALLELS

There is a line in Goethe's *Faust*, "Gefuhl ist alles" (Feeling is all), out of which a theory of aesthetics has been built. It was applied mostly to lyric poetry. It grew to differ from Wordsworth's idea that poetry was an emotion recollected in tranquility. It said that literature is an immediate expression of emotion. The idea of immediacy negates the idea of recollection or intellectualizing. The feeling or emotion is compelled, almost mystically, to reach its own words. The recording of feeling is paramount.

By the end of the nineteenth century, we have another German, Thomas Mann (whom Anna mentioned) saying that emotion by itself is unusable. Words are all. By 1910, the Austrian poet, Rilke, was saying that a poem is a distillation. Further in the century, the pendulum swung again and reason, the intellect, was claimed to be the destroyer of emotion. The forces of emotion, even the irrational, were more profound. Elemental energy changes the aspect of reality. Thus the Expressionists gave us "blue horses." In painting, Van Gogh and Gauguin had already deliberately transformed the objective world. Anti-realism based itself on emotion. Color and line became symbols of emotional states. When symbols devaluated the color and line from which they evolved, the expression became abstract as in Kandinsky (1866–1944), the Russian-born painter who was active in both France and Germany.

In England, where Lessing was maturing as an artist, it was in literature that Expressionism was coming into its own. In literature the relationship between the writer and another person or thing is initiated by a provisional impression based on the everyday world. It is almost immediately altered by the emotional state of the writer. Something new is being created. A union takes place between the original impression, the writer's emotion, and the behavior it has engendered. The emotion and the expression have become identical. If we realize that the emotions of a writer are pre-conditioned by the possibility of putting words on paper, we can get further help in our making of interpretations. We can reach the conclusion that the interpreter plays a role in creation.

It is at this point that the interpretations made by Mrs. Lessing's literary predecessors and her contemporaries gain in importance. Just as Mrs. Lessing was and still is a prolific writer, so is she a voluminous reader. It isn't too far-fetched to say every author she read, not only writers of literature but serious writers in many areas, influenced her. Textual analysis of *The Golden Notebook* appears to indicate the influence of certain writers. Their relative importance is, however, conditioned by a reader's "other reading." To avoid evaluating relative importance, the following list, obviously limited for the sake of space, is put in alphabetical order. The omission of a name does not preclude an "influence." For this reason, a bibliography is appended for the reader's guidance.

## BALZAC, HONORE DE (1799–1850)

In the spring of 1833 Balzac is said to have rushed into his sister's room and cried, "Congratulate me. I am just becoming a genius." His idea of the "reappearing character" had flashed - into his consciousness. Vautrin is one of his reappearing characters who plays the same role in *Le Pere Goriot* as he does in different settings in other novels. Proust followed along and used the same character to reveal a psychological characteristic. But Mrs. Lessing came along and gave the same character different names in the same book. This technique, used so successfully in *The Golden Notebook*, is not the only influence this famous French story-teller had upon Mrs. Lessing.

The creator of the *Human Comedy*, under which title Balzac collected some of his eighty books, has been called the Napoleon of literature. He has recently, in 1972, twelve years after the publication of *The Golden Notebook*, enjoyed a revival. Two new books, Bernard N. Schilling's *The Hero as Failure* and Charles Affron's *Patterns of Failure in "La Comedie humaine,"* point up the very **theme** Doris Lessing used a decade earlier. The subject of failure is as challenging as ever. Balzac revolted against the social system of his time that caused men to fail. His **theme** centered on how society corrupted morally immature men. Mrs. Lessing writes how morally immature men have brought failure to women.

## BECKETT, SAMUEL (1906- )

Although she is but thirteen years his junior, Mrs. Lessing is supposed to have been influenced by Beckett. We can be quite sure that Lessing was familiar with the work of this Irishman, who writes in French, long before the general public. Scarcely known until he was awarded the Nobel prize, he is still relatively obscure except in small theatre and academic circles where commentary about him is more prolific than he is. Beckett's trilogy, the three novels, *Molloy*, *Malone Dies*, and *The Unnamable*, are reminiscent of Balzac's idea of the "reappearing character." In Beckett it is not a case of a reappearing character for Molloy, Malone and Murphy are not differentiated in time and place as they would have been in Balzac. The absurdity of the world has increased since Balzac's France was its center. Beckett's world is post-Hiroshima. His novels show men sliding to lower levels. They are subjects of more and more disintegration including mental disintegration.

Malone writing in bed is hard to distinguish from Beckett just as Anna writing at her trestle table is nearly indistinguishable from Lessing. There is one big difference. Beckett found it necessary to break off every so often to make sure the reader knew the difference between the creator and the created. This was made unnecessary by Mrs. Lessing's clever literary device of the colored notebooks interleaved with the Free Women passages.

Becketts' novels, conceived without plot and executed sometimes without paragraphing or punctuation, are extremely difficult to read. He is a strict absurdist in both content and in formlessness. In his most famous play he created a world in which Godot never arrives

Although Mrs. Lessing despairs over the violence and misery of the world, she never envisions it "so empty that a solitary human being seems a monstrous intrusion." In Beckett, his mollusc clams up; in Doris Lessing, the crab sheds its shell. (In her later novel, *The Four-Gated City*, the character who says she must withdraw into her shell is truly mad.)

Both Lessing and Beckett seem to see eye-to-eye on the subject of dreams. Both admit that, though a dream may seem quite irrational in the light of day, there is logic behind it - a logic compelled by the dreamer. It was inevitable that dream situations appealed to them as a creative tool. Beckett once said to an interviewer, "The dream is pure drama. In a dream, one is always in mid-situation."

There is another important similarity between Samuel Beckett and Doris Lessing - their preoccupation with rooms, a predilection also shared with Virginia Woolf (as discussed below). With Beckett we have the analogy-room, womb. Beckett is said to have retained a terrible memory of life in his mother's womb. This was his "antenatal" memory. Throughout much of his writing Beckett asks why a man, once born, continues to be unable to grasp the why and wherefore of his existence. His old men are helpless foetuses. They fear the violence of a second birth. In death they will be expelled into the unknown.

Mrs. Lessing's characters seem to suggest a subconscious desire to return to the womb. They need warmth and protection. The feeling is akin to what psychologists call a "death wish."

Anna is frequently conscious of her being in a room. She has a desire to remind herself where she is. The pinning up of news items makes a room both anonymous and personal. This mixing of the anonymous and the personal is an aspect of the philosophical thinking of both Beckett and Lessing.

## DICKENS, CHARLES (1812–1870)

Dickens manipulated his readers into certain states. Given certain clues, the reader experiences certain emotions without having to suffer or act. He can enjoy the story and still be dependent or independent of its argument or advice. Pages of emotion and pages of persuasion lie side by side in both Dickens and Lessing. As his audience appreciated his concern for their fellowmen, so does Lessing's. If a reader listens in, he can discover his own times. Doris Lessing brings this somewhat unpopular Victorian stance up to date.

## ELIOT, T. S. (1888–1965)

Eliot directed his readers to certain attitudes of the twentieth century. Even though he insisted he was not sending signals, his readers get his message of unconcern, particularly in *The Waste Land*. Doris Lessing is not so haughty. She changes his unconcern of the concern into concern for the unconcern. She recognizes his anti-rhetoric as a mirror of honest rhetoric. If as a serious artist she uses rhetoric (persuasion) unabashedly, it is because she feels our times demand a strong prophylactic.

## HUXLEY, ALDOUS (1894–1963)

The author of *Point Counter Point* is famous for the catholicity of his taste, his enormous reading, and, towards the end of his life, for his interest in Yoga, extrasensory perception, and the expansion of learning, even if drug stimulated. Lessing bears, comparison, particularly in connection with her wide interest in science and psychology. She despairs for the world unless man learns more not only about his physical world but more about his mind. Mrs. Lessing has had at least one controlled experience with mescaline. Her investigations into the subconscious through psychiatry and her profound interest in dreams invite comparison with Huxley's experiments in his California home. Both writers presume a connection between neurotic behavior and artistic creation. In writing about Anna, a novelist, Mrs. Lessing may be said to have written a "patho-biography." Anna, herself, writing about her novelist Ella, also plays the role of a psychiatrist. She is Ella's Mother Sugar. Huxley, at the time of his death, and Mrs. Lessing with increasing interest, appear to await a breakthrough or at least a reformulation of psychological theory. In their writing both stress the meaning as well as the causes of behavior. They look to a time when illness and creativeness will no longer be confused as Freud admittedly confused them.

## KAFKA, FRANZ (1883–1924)

Like Anna, this Bohemian writer kept notebook diaries and like Anna he analyzed his dream world. Like Anna he had his tiger. As Anna had her grasshoppers, he had his cockroach. He was also haunted by the repetition of certain nightmares. In Mrs. Lessing's earlier series, *The Children of Violence*, Martha Quest is afraid in her dreams that she is going to be like her mother. This **theme** some find analogous to the ambitions of free women. They are driven to revolt out of fear of being like their mothers.

There is also a suggestion of similarity between Anna's views on romance and Kafka's. Kafka, as the repeated seeker of romance and repeated fugitive from marriage, was like the so-called founder of Existentialism, Kierkegaard, who also abandoned his fiance. It is seemingly safe to assume that Kafka rarely, if ever, experienced love-even though he seemed always to have plenty of sex, both free and paid for.

Although Kafka was sympathetic to the Zionists, he never became one. His Jewishness constantly reminded him of the Talmud from which he took the thought that he could not change the world. That is the concern of angels. Kafka seemed to be aware of something indestructible in himself - a something he wanted to think as an expression of God and yet, when he did, it seemed he was meeting Nietzsche's "dead God." When he explored evil, awake or asleep, he lacked Anna's hope. His forebodings were prophetic. He suffered when he saw humanism taking the place of his forebears' religious belief.

His understanding of the Russian revolution was like Anna's after she had left the Party. He saw the ideals of the revolution become shallower and muddier leaving a slime behind. Like Dostoyevski before him, and Anna after him, he saw socialism as almost hopeless but worth striving for.

Middle-class like Anna, he was sympathetic to the working class. As an insurance-claims clerk, he knew how bad things could get for the workman. In his case this sometimes caused collapse. Anna was tough but her Jewish friend Molly and her half-Jewish son, Tommy, were not.

## ROBBE-GRILLET, ALAIN (1922- )

An almost exact contemporary of Lessing, Robbe-Grillet begins his short novel *The Erasers*, after a conversation, "That's just the whole point...." One can't get much closer to the opening of *The Golden Notebook*.

Robbe-Grillet belongs to the group of so-called "new" French writers identified as Existentialists. Robbe-Grillet has departed from the main line as has Doris Lessing. Accordingly she seems to have more in common with him.

They both differentiate between objective reality and what appears to be real in literature. As a consequence, clock-time or calendar-time differs from literary sequences in time. They both distinguish between deep and surface structure. They present the reader with a surface story and expect him to get the deeper meaning from its arrangement-form.

Both novelists utilize repetition. Here the similarity is inexact. Robbe-Grillet's repetitions are frequently in precisely the same words. Sometimes they are but partial sequences - clues. His symbols are included in the repetitions and therefore take on greater proportions.

In both writers, symbols "grow." They are not casual embellishments but a deep part of the structure. They are what T. S. Eliot called "objective correlatives." Such a symbol is the crushing of the centipede in *Jealousy*. Like Mrs. Lessing's insects, the symbol can become, first rhythmic, then erotic. In both, the symbol is a stressing of different features of an event.

In Robbe-Grillet's *Jealousy*, the wife suffers from malaria attacks. In Lessing we have an outstanding malaria symbolism. In Robbe-Grillet, the mathematical symbols are rampant-isosceles triangles, trapezoids, rhomboids in proliferation. In Lessing, they are minimal - the five pointed star.

Lessing uses restraint. She strikes a golden mean concerning the allowance or disallowance of interior monologue and psychological analyses. She is influenced by the traditional as well as the avant-garde.

## SAND, GEORGE (MADAME AURORE DUDEVANT) (1804–1876)

If Mrs. Lessing's dates coincided with George Sand's, she might have called herself something like David Less. Born Aurore Dupin, married at eighteen to Dudevant, delivered of two children, she ran away in the fashion of Ibsen's Nora, with Jules Sandeau, who would have become her second husband but for the divorce provisions of the Napoleonic code.

She was to produce a hundred books, eighty of them novels. The publication of her correspondence is expected to run to twenty-five volumes, the last tentatively scheduled for 1983. Because of a flurry in the feminist movement, a movie of her life is shortly to be released with Jean-Luc Godard's wife as the star. Sand's own generation accused her of nymphomania as they would have accused any woman who took men as the men of her time took women. Literary giants, Henry James, Walt Whitman, Elizabeth Barret Browning, and Heine were among those who shouted her praises. The story of her life is not, however, the story of her loves and love stories.

She was also active politically. She was "effective minister of propaganda of the revolutionary Republic of 1848." This revolution, as we know, failed but the cry of the peasants around Nohant "Death to the Communists, death to George Sand!" continues to echo. By the time of the Paris commune of 1871, she held more conservative views yet still adhered to her commitment to the betterment of the world's less fortunate. Certain parallels to Lessing's emancipated heroines require no further comment.

## WOOLF, VIRGINIA (1882-1941)

Mrs. Woolf said she was going to portray women as they appeared in their relationship to men. This was a departure from the main stream of English literature where women usually appeared in their relationship to other women. She also said she was going to describe "men's blind spots." It is because of such statements that Mrs. Woolf is included among the forerunners of the current women's liberation movement.

Mrs. Lessing's free women are descendants from Mrs. Woolf's Bloomsbury heroines who become quite girlish in comparison.

Mrs. Lessing not only describes her women in their relationships to men but their relationships with men. Moreover, the Lessing relationships are most apt to be conflicts.

Let us compare Mrs. Woolf's well known "moments," moments made beautiful by sensory images associated with experience, and Anna's moments with Michael! Let us compare Mrs. Woolf's story of the old man releasing the pigeon when he sees his granddaughter with a young man (in releasing the pigeon, he is releasing his resentment) with Mrs. Lessing's pigeon stories - Paul's shooting the pigeons on the vlei and the old London char's burying the kicked pigeon!

Academic talk about "stream of consciousness" now seems dated. Certainly there has been a literary reaction in the form of the "objective writing" of the new French and the American novel of where the "action" is. Inner dialogue gave way to continuous dialogue. Mrs. Lessing, as has been indicated, stands midway between the two extremes.

Mrs. Woolf contended a writer needed a room of her own. With this sentiment Mrs. Lessing surely agrees but her sense of space has expanded with her world. Speleology is no longer limited to a study of caves. Symbolically, Anna's room has become a spacious room. Even so Mrs. Lessing's women must get out of their rooms - they take long night strolls through London's variant neighborhoods. Mrs. Woolf's rooms acquire a mood from the women (the housewives) who sat in them - indoors.

To both novelists, rooms are important. Rooms are home. Lessing makes repeated references to the room of her childhood in the farmhouse on the veld. Anna dreams in her rooms about the rooms of her life. Mrs. Lessing's realization that not only does an artist need a room but everybody needs a room has since been corroborated by scientific investigations. Scientifically, animals have a sense of territory which is linked with sexual maturity.

It is here worthwhile to remember that in the 1950's Mrs. Lessing, following Mrs. Woolf, seemed aware of what science has since substantiated. She felt that even though human beings were often destroying themselves, they were going to gain more control of their bodies. The senses might not always be limited to five. What is this sense of territory? Proxemics is the name currently given to the study of territory, man's spatial relationships. Psychiatrists and students of body language speak of "intimate distance," "keeping him at arm's length," and "not with a ten-foot pole."

Mrs. Woolf in her portraits keeps her readers at a distance. Mrs. Lessing has changed this. One walks around her sculptures. Hers is a theatre in the round. She has departed from the stream of consciousness concept where one steady pair of eyes views the world. She has expanded the literary technique so often called "the point of view" about whose uniformity Henry James was so concerned.

## YEATS, WILLIAM BUTLER (1865–1939)

This poet's lines

> **"Civilization is hooped together, brought**
> **Under a rule, under the semblance of peace,**
> **By manifold illusion"**

appears to be written ahead of the times. In 1960 Doris Lessing's definition of civilization still echoes Yeats. She wrote of the violence that lies beneath the semblance of peace. Her examples of illusions, both public and private, are manifold.

# THE GOLDEN NOTEBOOK

. . . . . . . . . . . . . . . . . . . . . . . . . . . . . . . . . . . . . . . . . . . . . . . . . . . . . . . . . . . . . . . .

Question: Why is Doris Lessing called a novelist of commitment?

Answer: It has been averred that Mrs. Lessing has made commitments in three major fields. She is first of all committed to the ideas that no one wins wars today and that civilians suffer as well as combatants. Secondly, she is committed to the concepts that human beings are more alike than they realize and that class distinctions are outdated. Lastly, she is committed to the belief that the world will go forward in spite of violence.

World War I overthrew the Russian Czar and the German Kaiser. World War II overthrew the Bolsheviks, put into power a new set of Communists, and overthrew the dictators Mussolini and Hitler. Wars that had once been fought to protect one's land, one's home, one's wife and children had grown so out of proportion that the women and children of both sides were the major victims.

Even earlier the English invaded Africa. The black man, his wife and children were beaten and are still being beaten. The white women who followed their husbands out of England watched the cruelty, grew sick with guilt, and are still sick. Mrs. Boothby is a typical example.

Anna is an upper-middle class writer whose father was a career Army colonel. Molly was an actress born into a working-class Jewish family. They were both "free women" devoted to reforming the world. Paul's father was armed with a British title. Ted was a scholarship student from the lower classes. Both were Oxford-trained and junior pilots in a war they considered a mockery. Marion was to the manor born and got herself arrested in youth demonstrations. Muriel was the housewife who poured over greasy copies of Women at Home. Neither could make their ambitious husbands happy. The twentieth-century wars have been expensive. Psychological aftermaths recognize none of the barriers of wealth or class.

Throughout *The Golden Notebook* Anna is portrayed as a boulder-pusher. Sisyphus, the original of the myth, is recalled at the outset. The struggle, two steps forward, one step back, against stupidity is fought relentlessly. Anna failed many times. Living in an age of violence she failed at marriage, she failed with her book, she failed with her child. These were steps backward. Yet at the end of the book, Anna is a wiser person. She has learned why her marriage failed, how to write a better book, and how to raise her child. Her fight against her own stupidity has paid off. The battle is not won but she has a commitment to keep on fighting. Such is the process. Such is the **theme** of *The Golden Notebook*: success in failure.

Question: Why is Doris Lessing considered an experimental novelist?

Answer. If for no other reason, Mrs. Lessing may be considered an experimental novelist because of the shape of *The Golden Notebook*. Her interest in the relationship of forms is both a forerunner and an outgrowth of the space age. *The Golden Notebook* is a universe of different stories. The characters are propelled from one story to another.

Literature has had plays within plays, fictional plots within fictional plots. Novels have been written as diaries. Balzac, said to have invented the reappearing character, was borrowing an idea from Homer.

Mother Sugar remarked to Anna that there had been many women before her who had earned the title of free woman and many women who had been artists. Nevertheless, to her claim that Anna was but one among many such figures, Anna pointed out with vehemence that no artist living in an age of bombs and rockets could be the same as her predecessors. The violent new world demanded new forms - spatial forms.

Mrs. Lessing puts space around her characters. She spaces their stories apart. She looks at them from the angles of the various notebooks. She lives a day to day life in London while she writes about Africa and Moscow. Then, like a Japanese flower arranger, she puts the tall and the short together - even adds a few symbolic stones - the kopjes of the veld. The eucalyptus trees of Africa are scented with the perfume of a London street-peddler's strawberries. The red notebook of revolution, the black of the new politics, the yellow of cowardice, the blue of disillusion are requirements in form. Such diversity is put together within a single framework, between the two covers of a book.

The space age has no precedent. The only way out of chaos is to experiment. The age of experimentation can only be represented by an experimental literature. The spatial arrangement of *The Golden Notebook* is such an experiment.

Question: Has Doris Lessing made any linguistic contribution?

Answer: Linguists used to be famous, particularly in America, for going around with tape recorders to learn new unwritten languages, speech variations in dialects, signals in bird-calls and grunts in animals. Many specialized branches of linguistic science are challenging investigators. One of these is popularly called visceral language or body language. It is in this area that Mrs. Lessing is noteworthy.

Julius Fast, in his 1970 book, *Body Language*, reported what a man, leaning against a fireplace with his thumbs in his belt and his fingers pointing down to his groin, was saying to the girl on the other side of the room. In *The Golden Notebook* written ten years earlier, Mrs. Lessing uses this same stance with which an American sends signals to Anna.

In a more recent volume, which is meticulously notated and documented, Body Time: Physiological Rhythms and Social Stress, irs author Gay Gaer Luce scientifically substantiates relationships very clearly indicated in Doris Lessing's fiction. The reasons why Anna's mouth went dry or her armpits grew cold and wet may be based on glandular study but the reasons why the glands behaved as they did were not new to Mrs. Lessing. The situation in which Anna found herself demanded description in as few words as possible. Every good English writer since the philosopher William of Ockham put forth his theory known as Occam's Razor in the fourteenth century, has made use of his maxim "That assumptions introduced to explain a thing must not be explained beyond necessity."

When Marion squints up her eyes and then pops them wide open, Mrs. Lessing is describing drunkenness. Every drinker squints when trying to think through the fumes of alcohol and then stares as if to attest his sobriety! When body language requires fewer words, body language communicates.

As has been said, Mrs. Lessing is not an innovator in this area. Some earlier masters of body language were greatly admired by her, namely, Thomas Mann, Beckett, Robbe-Grillet, and our own Jack Kerouac. She not only followed in a tradition, but also advanced the technique. Her wide reading in psychology enhanced her already acute powers of observation.

In the famous pigeon-kicking scene, the old lady is a red-faced virago. Her anger is the communication. The fifteen-year-old boys are chewing gum. The message is that they are too callous to emote. One of the boys lets out a "long, incredulous, jeering admiring whistle." The message is that in the big cities like London, the police have a problem.

The mouth is but one of the known sense-organs. Man can also communicate with his glands, with his "sense" of territory, with his ESP. Lessing's tentative hunches about "neo-homo" are gradually being confirmed by the scientists of the seventies.

# THE GOLDEN NOTEBOOK

Other literary comparisons may become topics for research. The following possibilities are again listed in alphabetical sequence to avoid subjective ranking.

Brecht, Bertolt (1898–1956). His view of the atomic age in relation to one's personal conscience affords comparison. His play *Galileo* is significant.

Camus, Albert (1913–1960). The new hero, a symbol of fallen humanity, is the subject of his novel, *The Stranger*. This type of solitary unattached person, as a recording consciousness, may be revisited in Lessing's Anna.

Dostoyevski, Fyodor (1821–1881). Mrs. Lessing's interest in revolutionary ideas and her anguish over the chaos of her world as subjects for literature are traceable to the Russian master who was jailed and exiled because of his politics.

Ibsen, Henrik (1828–1906). This Norwegian playwright is well known for his portrayal of emancipated women, namely Nora, Hedda Gabler, and Mrs. Alving.

James, Henry (1843–1916). His theory that a novel's real business is commitment is particularly relevant.

Joyce, James (1882–1941). In contrast to this Irishman, Mrs. Lessing, it has been contended, is too dependent on memory at the expense of imagination. This theory is subject to argument from both aesthetic and psychological viewpoints.

Kerouac, Jack (1922–1969). This famous American portrayer of hippies, openly admired by Mrs. Lessing, suggests comparison based on Anna's love of jazz and her sensitivity to body language.

Mann, Thomas (1875–1955). The conflict between the needs of the artist and the "repressive" demands of society were one of this writer's chief concerns. His interest in dreams is another subject for comparison. *Death in Venice*, recently released as a film, is noteworthy.

Nabokov, Vladimir (1899– ). His heroes and heroines, like Doris Lessing's, give us their experiences in time and backward time. They attempt to surmount time. Nabokov is also intrigued by the possibility of mutations still coming in the human species so that men can enjoy additional senses. This is the type Nabokov calls the "neo homo."

Orwell, George (1903–1950). Because of his projection *1984*, Mrs. Lessing's novel *The Four-Gated City*, which she wrote immediately following *The Golden Notebook*, is interesting because in it she describes a nuclear bombout of England.

Sartre, Jean-Paul (1905- ). The famous French existentialist, who refused the Nobel prize, wrote *Nausea* in diary form. It is a story of a writer who mercilessly lists his feelings concerning the world around him.

Svevo, Italo (pseudonym for Ettore Schmitz - 1861–1928). Befriended and encouraged by James Joyce, he wrote *Oblomov*, a book increasing at long last in literary prestige because of its early recognition of the stupidity of war - one of Mrs. Lessing's dominant themes.

# BIBLIOGRAPHY

· · · · · · · · · · · · · · · · · · · · · · · · · · · · · · · · · · · · · · · · · · · · · · · · · · · ·

## PERIODICALS

Adams, Robert M. "The Sense of Verification: Pragmatic Commonplaces about Literary Criticism." *Daedalus* (Winter, 1972).

Bannon, B. A. "Portrait of Doris Lessing." *Publishers' Weekly*, 196 (Dec. 2, 1969), 51–4.

Bayley, John. "Bloomsbury's Bequest (Virginia Woolf)." *The Guardian* (Manchester, England, Nov. 4, 1972).

Bliven, Naomi. *Review of The Golden Notebook.* The New Yorker (June 1, 1962).

Bowers, Fashion. "Ubiquitous Anglo-Saxon." *Saturday Review*, 44 (March 25, 1961), 25.

Dangerfield, George. "Novelists as Reporters (A review of Mrs. Lessing's *In Pursuit of the* English)". *Nation*, 192 (April 15, 1961), 324–5.

Davie, Donald. "The Rhetoric of Emotion." *Times Literary Supplement* (London, September 299, 1972).

Drabble, Margaret. "Cassandra in a World Under Siege." *Ramparts* 10 (Feb. 1972), 50–4.

Graver, Lawrence. Review of Lessing's *The Temptation of Jack Orkney.* *New York Times Book Review* (Oct. 29, 1972).

____. "The Commonplace Book of Doris Lessing (a review of *Children of Violence*, Vol. III & IV)." *New Republic* 154 (April 2, 1966), 27–9.

Hardwick, E. "Four-Gated City Ends with a Catastrophe." *Vogue* 174 (July, 1969), 50.

Hicks, Granville. "All About a Modern Eve." *Saturday Review* 49 (April 2, 1966), 31–2.

Howe, Florence. "Doris Lessing's Free Woman." *Nation*, 200 (January 11, 1965), 34–7.

____, editor of excerpts from interview: "Talk with Doris Lessing." *Nation*, 204 (March 6, 1967), 311–13.

Howe, Irving. "Neither Compromise nor Happiness." *New Republic* (Dec. 15, 1962).

Jonas, Gerald. "Visceral Learning I and II (Profile of Dr. Neal E. Miller)" *New Yorker* (Aug. 19 and Aug. 26, 1972).

Lessing, Doris. "Being Prohibited." *New Statesman and Nation* (London, April 21, 1956).

Litwak, Leo. "Rolfing, Aikido, Hypnodramas, Psychokinesis, and Other Things Beyond the Here and Now." *N. Y. Times Magazine* (Dec. 17, 1972).

Locke, Richard. "In Praise of Doris Lessing" (a review of *The Temptation of Jack Orkney*). N. Y. *Times* (Sat. Oct. 21, 1972).

Lydon, S. "Back of the Book." *Ramparts*, 8 (Jan. 1970), 48.

Manning, Margaret. "A Collision with Life's Conflicts (a review of *The Temptation of Jack Orkney* by Doris Lessing)." *Boston Globe* (Nov. 6, 1972).

Miller, Charles. "Kaffir-lover in Rhodesia (a review of Mrs. Lessing's *Going Home*)." *Saturday Review* 51 (March 23, 1968), 45–6.

Newquist, Roy. "An Interview with Doris Lessing." *Counterpoint* (Rand McNally & Co., pp. 414–424, 1964).

Rosenthal, Michael. "The High Priestess of Bloomsbury (Virginia Woolf)." *N. Y. Times Book Review* (Nov. 5, 1972).

Rycroft, Charles. "The Artist as Patient." *Times Literary Supplement* (London, Sept. 22, 1972).

Taubman, Robert. "Free Women." *New Statesman* (April 20, 1962).

Thompson, John. "The Four-Gated City, a Review (also reviews and compares Nabokov's *Ada*)." *Harper's Magazine* (Sept., 1969).

## BOOKS

Baumer, Franz, tr. by *Abraham Farbstein*. Franz Kafka. N. Y.: Fred. Unger Pub. Co., 1971.

Bree, Germaine. *Jalousie: New Blinds or Old*. New Haven: Yale University Press, French Studies #24, 1960.

Brewster, Dorothy. *Doris Lessing*. New York: Twayne, 1965.

Burgess, Anthony. *The Novel Now*. New York: W. W. Norton, 1967.

Chesler, Phyllis. *Women and Madness*. New York: Doubleday & Co., 1972.

Cruickshank, John (Editor). *The Novelist as Philosopher*. New York: Oxford University Press, 1962.

Daiches, David. *The Novel and the Modern World*. Chicago: University of Chicago Press, Revised 1960.

Fast, Julius. *Body Language*. New York: M. Evans & Co., Inc., 1970.

Foss, Martin. *Symbol and **Metaphor** in Human Experience*. Princeton, N. J.: Princeton University Press, 1949.

Hall, E. T. *Man's Image in Medicine and Anthropology*. New York: International Universities Press, 1963.

____. *The Silent Language*. New York: Doubleday & Co., 1959.

LeSage, Laurent: *The French New Novel*. Penn: The Pennsylvania State University Press, 1962.

Luce, Gay Gaer. *Body Time: Physiological Rhythms and Social Stress*. New York: Random House, 1971.

Robbe-Grillet, Alain. *For a New Novel - Essays on Fiction*, translated by Richard Howard. New York: Grove Press, 1965.

Stoltzfus, Ben F. *Alain Robbe-Grillet and the New French Novel*. Illinois: Southern Illinois Press, 1964.

Weightman, J. C. *The Novelist as Philosopher*. New York: Oxford University Press, 1962.